DokuWiki:
A Wiki for
Software Developers

By Whil Hentzen

Edited by Ted Roche

Hentzenwerke Publishing, Inc.

Published by:
Hentzenwerke Publishing, Inc.
PO Box 170343
Milwaukee WI 53217

Hentzenwerke books are available at Amazon.com and directly through the
publisher. Contact us at:
414.332.9876
www.hentzenwerke.com
books@hentzenwerke.com

DokuWiki: A Wiki for Software Developers
By: Whil Hentzen
Technical Editor: Ted Roche
Cover Art: Todd Gnacinski

ISBN: 978-1-930919-16-7

Manufactured in the United States of America.

Chapter List

Table of Contents

About the Team

Whil Hentzen

Whil Hentzen fills the role of "player-coach" at Hentzenwerke Publishing, a 20 year old Milwaukee-based publisher that specializes in titles covering high-end software development and, more recently, the migration of Windows developers and users to Linux.

Whil started out life as a custom software developer using dBASE II (he still has the original 8 1/2 x 11 grey binder of documentation, much to the chagrin of his kids, who will likely have to throw it out upon his demise), and switched to FoxPro in 1990. As an independent Fox developer, he billed over 15,000 hours in the 90's, including the requisite "1,000 hours in 3 months" Y2K emergency gig while recovering from leg surgery.

During that time, he presented more than 70 papers at conferences throughout North America and Europe, edited FoxTalk, Pinnacle Publishing's high end technical journal for 7 years, and hosted the Great Lakes Great Database Workshop since 1994. In 1999, Microsoft contracted with Whil to co-author the Certification Exam for Visual FoxPro 6.0 Distributed Applications, which has since been taken by thousands of developers to help them achieve Microsoft Certified Solution Developer credentials. He was a Microsoft Most Valuable Professional from 1995 through 2003 for his contributions to the FoxPro development community, and received the first Microsoft Lifetime Achievement Award for Visual FoxPro in 2001.

He started writing in order to develop credentials to bolster his software development career. His first book, Rapid Application Development with FoxPro, showed up in 1993, and seven more have appeared since. He started Hentzenwerke Publishing in 1996 to self-publish a specialized volume on software development, and then began producing Visual FoxPro books when the major publishers abandoned the market in 1998. Sensing the impending acceptance of Linux on the desktop and anticipating a coming demand for custom business applications on those Linux desktops, he turned his attentions to Linux in 2002, and now has a dozen narrowly targeted Linux and open source books available. Despite being HQ'd in Whil's house, HWP's backlist now numbers close to 50, with some 70 authors and editors worldwide on the payroll.

He currently splits his time between freelance custom development with Visual FoxPro and a host of open source tools such as MySQL, PHP, and Python, and running the publishing side of the biz.

Whil has a B.S. in Mechanical Engineering from Rose-Hulman Institute of Technology, named as the United States' top independent engineering school every year since 1999 by U.S. News & World Report. He served on RHIT's Commission on the Future from 1993 to 1998.

He currently spends his copious amounts of spare time with his five kids and volunteering for the local school district. An avid distance runner, he has logged over 55,000 miles lifetime, plus another 60,000 on the bike and in the pool. As old age and common sense have closed the door on short distance competitions, he has

Hentzenwerke Publishing, Inc.
books@hentzenwerke.com • www.hentzenwerke.com

turned his attentions to adventure races. Evidently common sense is still in short supply.

You can reach Whil at whil@whilhentzen.com or at 414.332.9876.

Ted Roche

Ted Roche learned to program BASIC on a PDP-4 at the age of 15. He was conferencing and IM'ing on the Dartmouth Time Sharing System in the late 1970s. (IM and chat rooms are old. So's Ted.) He shipped his first commercial app in 1978, which ran on a WANG 2200. His first public domain software was a quad-density Epson printer driver for the Commodore 64 GEOS operating system, hand-coded in 6502 assembler. Amigas were his favorite computers, although PCs are getting better now that they've been replaced with smartphones. He ran the electrical plant on a nuclear-powered ballistic missile submarine until the Russians gave up, and then there wasn't any challenge in it any more. He has coded with "ohs."

Ted Roche is the owner of Ted Roche & Associates, LLC, a software development and consulting company based in Contoocook, New Hampshire USA. TR&A develops and maintains data-intensive web sites and rich-client (VFP) applications for clients in a range of industries from wholesale commodities to produce to financial services, manufacturing and insurance. Software at TR&A is produced in the presence of nuts. A nine-time Microsoft Most Valuable Professional, Ted now spends his time developing Free / Open Source solutions using Linux, Apache, MariaDB, PostgreSQL, PHP and Ruby. If you'd like to contact Ted for help on your project, his contact information can be found at www.tedroche.com.

Ted is author of Essential SourceSafe, co-author of the award-winning Hacker's Guide to Visual FoxPro trilogy, and a contributor to five other FoxPro books. He wrote 50 monthly Q&A columns for "FoxPro Advisor" and lead articles for that magazine and much-missed FoxTalk technical journal. After serving as lead author for the FoxPro Distributed exam (along with fellow lead author Whil Hentzen), Ted passed the tests to be a Microsoft Certified Solution Developer (in the Visual Studio 6 era) and Microsoft Certified System Engineer (Windows NT). He has previously held certifications in MySQL 4 and 5, First Responder, Senior Lifesaver, CPR, NASDS SCUBA diver, Throttleman and Shutdown Reactor Operator.

Since 2004, Ted has focused on Open Source web development, working primarily in Ruby on Rails and PHP with the related Apache, Linux, PostgreSQL, HTML5 and CSS3 technologies. He is a Certified Developer in MySQL 5.0. He served as Fearless Leader of the Greater New Hampshire Linux User Group for several years. He has been inducted into the Association of Computing Machinery as a Senior Member. He has paid his dues. In 2013, Ted was awarded the FoxPro Lifetime Achievement Award.

Downloads 'N Other Stuff

Before we get started, a couple of notes about what's inside, and what additional resources are available.

Source Code

The source code consists of one big ZIP file that consists of separate ZIP files for each chapter. Check out the "README.TXT" files inside each chapter's ZIP file for details. Note that not every chapter will have a file.

To download, navigate to www.hentzenwerke.com and click on "Download". Follow the instructions from there.

Screen Shots

The screen shots and URLs throughout this book were current as of the writing and/or printing. Depending on when you are reading this, they might have changed. ("Might have"? Of course they have!) See the errata on our Web site, http://www.hentzenwerke.com, for updates as we find them.

Revisions

Towards helping you make sure you've got the latest version of this book.

History

Version	Date	Synopsis	Author
1.0.0	03/31/18	Original	WH

New version

The newest version of this document can be downloaded at www.hentzenwerke.com. Click on "Download".

Hentzenwerke Publishing, Inc.
books@hentzenwerke.com • www.hentzenwerke.com

1: The Introduction You Have To Read

Wherein I describe why a software developer needs a wiki, why I chose DokuWiki over all of the other guys, what I'm going to cover in this book, and how to pronounce 'DokuWiki' the way all the cool kids do.

I had a problem. I'm a freelance software developer based in Milwaukee, WI, which is, to borrow a line from Mal in Josh Whedon's Firefly, at the corner of 'No' and 'Where'. In other words, my customers are everywhere but Milwaukee - East Coast, West Coast, Europe, Far East, why, even a couple in that strange, foreign land known as "Texas."

The Problem

For years, I have developed specifications via an OpenOffice.org document - I'd write something and send it to my contact at the customer. They'd review it, mark it up, perhaps pass it by their folks, and then send it back, hopefully having turned revision marks on so I could see their changes. Then I'd update the document again, send it to them, and so on and so forth. We'd use email and the telephone to flesh out concepts and ideas, and occasionally I'd visit them, but the document we passed back and forth served as the ultimate arbiter of what we'd discussed through other channels. Most of the time I'd also create a prototype of what was being described in the specification, and send them a program.

Worked great.

Eventually, though, I ran into situations that this process didn't address well. There were scenarios where more than one person wanted to work on the spec at the same time. Often, once coding started, and always, once pieces of the application were being delivered, changes to the application were made - meaning the spec was now out of touch with reality. I did my best to keep the document updated, but this was time-consuming and, frankly, no one but me ever looked at the spec after it was accepted.

The Solution

A better vehicle for sharing information was needed. Enter the wiki.

A wiki is a program that resides on a Web site which allows visitors to edit the pages. Changes made to the pages are tracked through a version control system where users can see what older versions of the pages looked like and who made the changes. It's a wonderful tool for collaborating on the creation of documents as well as an excellent repository for knowledge acquired by a group of people. The Wikipedia, www.wikipedia.org, is probably the most well-known wiki.

With the increasing popularity of wikis, people use the term 'wiki' to both define the software as well as the web site it runs. In this book, the distinction - when I'm talking about the DokuWiki software and when I'm talking about the wiki - should be clear.

Choosing

A wiki is a type of program. Just as there are many brands of word processors - such as Microsoft Word and OpenOffice.org - there are many brands of wikis, and choosing the right one can be difficult. Back when I started this wiki-quest (circa 2008, perhaps?), I'd taken a look at the Wiki Matrix (www.wikimatrix.com) and gotten overwhelmed quickly. It currently has 141 wikis to compare and contrast. I had several non-negotiable requirements:

1. Installable on a shared web host
    • I didn't want to have to deal with hosting on a local box, require esoteric functionality, strange language runtimes or database engines not always provided with inexpensive hosting accounts.

2. Restricted access
    • While the general concept of a 'wiki' is public access, for this use, I had to be able to restrict access to a limited number of users, in a way that my customers would feel comfortable with - since it was their information that was going on the wiki.

3. Either PHP or Python based
    • I didn't want to learn Java or C++ or Lisp.

Additionally, I didn't want to deal with a 'toy' wiki that would be good for a couple of users on a local machine, but wouldn't scale well for thousands of pages and perhaps a dozen or more users. I didn't see myself using a wiki for scope larger than that, but didn't want to unnecessarily limit myself either.

Using the customized search tool on the WikiMatrix site, I'd eventually narrowed my list down to MoinMoin and MediaWiki. MoinMoin is Python based while MediaWiki uses PHP. They both can use MySQL as the backend database to store content.

MoinMoin's installation quickly involved more work than I wanted to invest. To be fair, part of the complexity is because it's really flexible. But the questions came fast and furious - and I didn't have enough background info to make informed decisions. CGI or Standalone? Apache on Linux? Mac? Windows? IIS? WebLogic? Apache with ModWSGI? Or ModPython? Twisted Web? FastCGI on Lighttpd? Once you choose one of these, then the real work begins.

Too much work for me, at the time.

While MediaWiki's installation was trivial compared to MoinMoin:

```
root# yum install mediawiki
```

it didn't have the ability to restrict access to a selected group of users. They're very upfront about it - MediaWiki is for public collaboration. However, that means their tools for using it as a private wiki are somewhat limited and convoluted to use. For example, in the "Preventing Access" topic, they say "Schools and other institutions may want to block all edits not from a few specified IP address ranges. To do so, all other ranges must be blocked. The only way to do this at present without modifying the code is to go to Special:Blockip and systematically block every one of the 65,536 CIDR Class B ranges that you don't want to be able to edit."

Ugh. So, again, at the time, MediaWiki was a no-go for me.

And the Winner Is...

While I was wrestling with these conundrums, I stumbled upon (not literally!) DokuWiki, billed as "aimed at creating documentation of any kind. It is targeted at developer teams, workgroups and small companies." Bingo!

It's easy to install locally or on a shared Web host: it took five minutes to get a five page wiki up and running, and another five to restrict access both via IP and through a login mechanism. It's also available for installation directly from popular distributions like Ubuntu.

It's written in PHP.

There are dozens of templates and hundreds of plugins that customize and extend the base engine.

And although its data store is simple text files, the engine is built to be able to handle tens of thousands of pages and access by dozens of users. While this may not be suitable for the specifications for an airline ticketing system or a replacement for the U.S. Internal Revenue Service tax collection software, it's fine for the 500 to 4,000 hour-long systems I write.

In fact, Andreas Gohr, the author, specifically used flat files instead of a database for a reason. He says, "DokuWiki was designed to hold documentation of all kinds. So what do you do when your database or your web server is down and the documentation to bring it up again is only accessible through this web server or database? Yikes! So DokuWiki stores all this vital information as plain text which is always readable, even if you only have some tape backups left of your beloved server."

Why a Book?

As I worked with DokuWiki, I figured it might be helpful if I wrote down what I did and share it with others. At this point, some may point out, "Ummm, there is already a wiki for DokuWiki - you should add your material there!" Others may offer, "Well, you're still talking about a wiki? If you feel the existing DokuWiki wiki is lacking, why not create your own wiki Web site?"

Fair enough.

First of all, let me make clear that I think the existing DokuWiki wiki is excellent. It really is - and time reading through it is time well spent. Considering all of the software I've used over the years, the DokuWiki wiki is way better than most - clearly laid out, easy to use, easy to find things, chock full of information.

But it's also good to have access to a different point of view. One of the first manuals I used was the dBASE II documentation. In 1981. While it was head and shoulders above anything else at the time, it still suffered from tunnel vision. They would use the same example in multiple help topics - an approach that failed miserably when (1) you didn't understand that example, or (2) there was an error in the example. Not everyone learns the same way. Thus, much better to have a couple different examples to provide varying viewpoints.

Second, I wanted to support the DokuWiki community. For some odd reason, having a book on the shelf (actually, that should be 'a book on Amazon', since bookstores these days are too full of music and stationary and stuffed animals to be bothered with carrying, of all things, books) adds legitimacy to a piece of software. It means that another company felt strongly enough about an application that they devoted resources to producing a book for it.

And third, there are those folks who prefer to read material while off-line. You know - in an armchair with a glass of cold milk and a couple of chocolate chip cookies. This is true more for 'concept' books than books that are simply syntax reference books - and this DW book has buckets of concept-oriented material that is perfect for reading in a hammock on a lazy Sunday afternoon with nary a computer in sight.

The downside to a book is that once it hits the printer... well, it's more difficult to change it than, oh, say, a wiki. I'm not going to sweat this point. Since this book was updated in late 2017, the book will be fresh for a while. More importantly, many of the concepts will be true even as subsequent releases are produced.

So this is my guide to you, a fellow software developer, on how to use DokuWiki to collaborate on software specifications and other related documents.

Let's do it!

The Road Ahead

Here's the setting for this book: picture a Saturday afternoon in winter. You're in the upper Midwest - it's been snowing since October. So the sky is bright blue, there's 3 1/2 foot of snow on the ground outside, cars are doing more sliding than driving down the minimally maintained village streets and the occasional power walkers are motoring past in full cold-weather gear, mittens and hats pulled on tight.

You've come over to learn about this DokuWiki software that I've been raving about on the local user group's mailing list. We're settled in my office for the afternoon, sitting in front of a pair of widescreen monitors, keyboards and mice at the ready, hot chocolate steaming away in mugs, and the Cream reunion concert at Royal Albert Hall playing softly in the background. I'm going to give you the nickel tour of how to install and use DokuWiki, and once you're comfortable with the basics, we'll discuss advanced DokuWiki administration and usage, tips and tricks. We might even try our hand at solving all of the world's problems before the sun disappears from office's western window.

This book is the written version of what will transpire this afternoon. The first couple of chapters are aimed at getting a basic wiki up and running. We'll install DW on a local machine (as opposed to a production server or a third-party host), so you can practice. Then we'll repeat the steps on a production server.

Next, we'll do some basic customization and configuration. After discussing tne basics of what a wiki page looks like, we'll do a few quick customizations, examine the installer in detail, and then discuss the important configuration options.

Third, we'll look at the wiki from the user's point of view. First, exploring usage, editing, and page formatting. Then explaining how the wiki versioning works – user changes, revisions, and drafts.

Fourth step on our journey are a couple of stand-alone chapters, dealing with templates and plugins. You can skip these if you like, but a quick overview will make sure you're not overlooking things that you'll want to know about right away.

The second last chapter in the book discusses deploying your wiki pages and upgrading the DW code when a new version is released.

Finally, and this is the good part, the last chapter pulls it all together. So far we've just talked about the wiki itself. But the title of this book is "A Wiki for Software Developers"

While I've endeavored to make the examples up to this point relevant specifically to the task at hand, they've still been more of an afterthought than the main focus. Now let's talk about writing, er, collaborating on software document, using this brand new widget in our utility belt as our primary tool.

What we've set up is the infrastructure that's well suited for developer documentation. The trouble is that, unlike, say, accounting, where there's a generally accepted method to doing a balance sheet, there isn't a single 'generally accepted practices' for software documentation. Everyone does it their own way. This last chapter provides a smorgasbord of items that you can pick and choose from as your particular circumstance, together with details of why you might or might not want to include them.

How to Pronounce (and Abbreviate) "DokuWiki"

DokuWiki mailing list member Jon Schneider posted a question about pronouncing DokuWiki years back. His reasoning was that he was about to sell it to other members of his team, and he wanted to get off on the right foot by pronouncing it correctly.

C'mon, 'fess up. I bet a few of you have been wondering the same thing. "DOCK-you"? Or "do-COO"? Or "DOE-kuh"? Or maybe some combination in between?

The correct answer is "DOE-coo". "DOE" as in "donut" and 'coo' as in 'cool'. Here's why.

Andi says "Doku is short for "Dokumentation" – the German word for documentation (and pronounced DOE-coo...) I'm from Germany so this was the very first working title..." He adds, "Most Americans tend to speak it like DocuWiki (like in document)." So now you know.

As an aside, I'll frequently be using "DW" as the abbreviation throughout the rest of this book, and will be referring to users of the wiki as 'visitors'.

That's all for now. Enjoy the ride.

Hentzenwerke Publishing, Inc.
books@hentzenwerke.com • www.hentzenwerke.com

Hentzenwerke Publishing, Inc.
books@hentzenwerke.com • www.hentzenwerke.com

2: Before We Begin

As developers, we always want to get started right away. Fire up the software, start poking a sharp stick here and there. But we really need a bit of background first, to understand what's under the hood, understand a bit about how Web Servers, and, more specifically, how DokuWiki works, and get acquainted with the file structures underneath.

Some tools we use with development are pretty much plug and play – we install them and begin using them, living in their environment, and not really needing to know much about the outside world other than, perhaps, where your data is stored.

We're going to want to know a bit more about the bigger world here.

Do I Need to be a PHP Programmer?

DokuWiki is written in PHP. Do you need to know how PHP works? Heck no.

You can go a long way with DokuWiki without knowing a line of PHP code. But it's helpful if you know a little - at least enough to be dangerous. You won't necessarily write any code, but being able to look at a set of PHP files and understand generally what's going on would help you be a better administrator. Here are a few things you should know about PHP.

PHP is a programming language, like BASIC, C++ or FoxPro. To process PHP programs in a web server, you need to register the PHP interpreter with the server. When the web server receives a request for a page with a .php extension, the server sends that page through the PHP interpreter, which processes it, creates output and turns the output over to the Web server which, in return, sends the output (plus, perhaps, more stuff) back to the browser of the requesting visitor.

PHP programs are simply text files, modifiable in any text editor. Anything enclosed within PHP delimiters is run through the PHP interpreter; anything outside is ignored. Generally, each statement or function is terminated with a semi-colon.

```
<?php
some_php_statement_or_command;
some_php_function();
?>
```

PHP can be embedded in an HTML code block, like so:

```
*** my_first_php_page.php
<body>
<h1>Hello World!</h1>
<?php
some_php_statement_or_command;
=some_php_function();
?>
<p><b>More basic HTML, in bold</b>
<?php
```

```
another_php_statement;
=another_php_function();
?>
</p>
</body>
```

Note that these examples are just descriptive, not functional. For files that end with PHP code, the closing tag ("?>") is strongly discouraged. It is not required by PHP. Not including it prevents trailing whitespace from being accidentally injected into the output.

Do I Need to Know How to Admin a Web Server?

Again, no. However, knowing a couple of things about administering a Web server will make your life easier. How many times have we heard Doc McCoy exclaim to Kirk, "Dammit Jim, I'm a programmer, not a systems administrator!" Well, OK, we never did, but if he was in our shoes, he would have. There are three important concepts of how the Web server works that will help you in the basic setup and configuration of DokuWiki that I'll discuss now: home directories, default documents and virtual folders.

Home Directory

First, there is the concept of a home directory. A Web server is simply a piece of software that waits for requests for files from a visitor (via their browser). Once the Web server receives a request, it'll look in it's home directory ('root folder') for that content. This home directory is identified in the Web server's configuration. On IIS, this folder is c:/inetpub/wwwroot while on Apache on Red Hat/Fedora it's set in /etc/http/conf/httd.conf's DocumentRoot command to /var/www/html.

Default Document

Second is the concept of a default document. If the user explicitly names a file in a Web browser address bar, that file is delivered, like so:

```
http://www.example.com/somefile.html
```

What if the user doesn't name a file? In other words, how does a Web server know what page to dish up when you simply navigate to 'www.example.com'? Enter the default document. Unbeknownst to the vast majority of Web surfers, a Web server is configured to automatically look for files with specific names if not otherwise instructed. When you install IIS, IIS's default document is automatically defined as 'default.htm' while Apache's default document out of the box is 'index.html'. These can be changed just like the root folder can be.

Furthermore, you can have multiple default documents defined - and in a specific order of priority; if one isn't found, the Web server will automatically look for the next document, and then the next, and so on. This is particularly handy when you want to have a PHP script be the default document. Setting 'index.php' as your highest-priority default document means that if you have an 'index.php' file in your document root, it'll automatically be executed. If 'index.php' doesn't exist, then the next default document, say, 'index.html', will be. DokuWiki takes advantage of this functionality, as you'll see shortly.

Virtual Folders

Third is the concept of virtual folders. When entering a URL, the visitor can include a path - elsewhere - to specify a subdirectory under the root folder. For example, a visitor might navigate to

```
http://www.example.com/customer_one/sales_presentations/listing.htm
```

to go to "Customer One's" listing of sales web pages while

```
http://www.example.com/customer_two/financial_results/index.htm
```

would do the same for Customer Two for their financial results. Web servers can be configured with 'virtual folders' that provide shortcuts to folders deep in the directory structure.

A virtual folder of 'onesales' might be mapped to 'customer_one/sales_presentations', so a visitor could enter

```
http://www.example.com/onesales/listing.htm
```

or

```
http://www.example.com/c2fin/index.htm
```

Furthermore, virtual folders can be mapped to their own URLs. Thus, visitors to Customer One's files might actually just navigate to

```
http://www.cust_one.com
```

and visitors to Customer Two's files would enter

```
http://www.cust_two.com
```

in their browser, none of them being any the wiser that they're all ending up somewhere deep within www.example.com's Web site.

You can use these concepts to create multiple wikis on a single Web site.

Windows vs. Linux

If you're a Windows developer, you may be disconcerted by the great, big, beautiful world outside the grasp of Redmond. This software, and this book, are a couple of examples. Ne'er fear - most open source software is built on the Linux platform, and if you're interested in open source, you only need to learn a bit about Linux. In fact, getting involved with an Open Source application like DokuWiki is an excellent way to dip your toe into the Open Source world without getting completely wet.

I'm flipping back and forth between Windows and Linux to write this book, and I'm using DokuWiki on both a Windows workstation and a Linux Web server. As a result, Windows folks might be a bit confused by some of the nomenclature and conventions they run into. Here are a couple of quick tips to help you navigate through some of the differences.

First, the forward slash indicates a folder. Why Microsoft programmers decided to use the backslash - the character used to initiate escape sequences in the UNIX world a decade before any 'softie had finished high school - to separate folders is beyond comprehension. We'll never know, and I digress. In Linux, folder hierarchies are separated with a forward slash.

Files that begin with a period are hidden from normal view. These are typically system or configuration files. I like to know what's going on so I keep the "Show Hidden Files" option in my file manager checked and that's what you'll see in screen shots in this book; the next Linux system you look at might not.

Linux doesn't rely on extensions to the extent that Windows does. The operating system knows what files are without depending on the extension. Thus, COPYING and README and VERSION (as well as .htaccess) are all understood by the file manager to be plain text files.

Web Site Files Location

If you've already built Web sites, you can probably skip this step, but you may want to read it anyway, just to make sure we're all using the same language and you understand the conventions I'm following. Since Web sites are like potato chips - no one can have just one - create a place where all of your Web sites will reside. I have a folder on my file server named "Sites" (clever, huh?). The Web server's root folder points to this /Sites folder. Under the /Sites folder, there are, for each Web site, the following folders:

```
/Sites/AlgorithmHeaven
/Sites/Hentzenwerke
/Sites/HentzenHause
/Sites/SoftwareMuscle
/Sites/WhilHentzen
```

and so on.

Since a customer Web site goes on my consultant's Web site, www.whilhentzen.com, I create folders for each customer under my main site, like so:

```
/Sites/WhilHentzen/cust_one
/Sites/WhilHentzen/cust_two
/Sites/WhilHentzen/cust_three
```

The wiki for Customer One goes in the cust_one folder, the wiki for Customer Two goes into cust_two, and so on.

You'll see in a moment that navigating to one of the customer's Web sites is then just a matter of

```
http://localhost/WhilHentzen/cust_one
```

because localhost will be pointed to /Sites when we configure the Web server.

DokuWiki Files Location

Next, you'll want a place for the DokuWiki files you're going to be using. DokuWiki comes in a single compressed file, but you'll most likely want to incorporate templates that alter the appearance (and, to some extent, the functionality) of DokuWiki, and plugins that provide additional functionality. So you may find yourself with a whole slew of files before you know it.

I have a folder named 'dw_masters' that I keep in my /Sites folder, alongside of the folders for each Web site.

```
/Sites/AlgorithmHeaven
/Sites/dw_masters/dokuwiki_source
/Sites/dw_masters/plugin_one
/Sites/dw_masters/plugin_two
/Sites/dw_masters/template_one
/Sites/HentzenHause
/Sites/HentzenWerke
/Sites/SoftwareMuscle
/Sites/WhilHentzen
```

and so on. Note that dw_masters only resides on my development Web server, for ease of access. I **don't** copy it to the production Web server!

The DokuWiki wiki

The DokuWiki wiki is a wonderful resource. Instead of repeating the entire URL throughout the book, I'll just use the name of the specific page. So a reference to

```
install:unpacking
```

can be accessed through the URL:

```
http://www.dokuwiki.org/install:unpacking
```

3: Windows/Development Quick Install

The goal of this chapter is to guide you through a simple DokuWiki installation from start to finish. We'll start by getting your environment ready. Then we'll download the software and install it on a Windows development machine, examine the user interface, and create and save your first wiki page. If you're using Linux, move on to the next chapter where I'll discuss installing DokuWiki on a Linux Web Server.

One of the features that attracted me to DokuWiki is the ease of installation. This chapter is 20 pages long, but the installation itself only takes a few minutes. I suggest that you do a 'throwaway' install first - run through all the steps in the first two chapters of this book, using a test site that you can get rid of when you're done experimenting. DokuWiki's architecture makes it easy to do so - all you have to do is delete the folder containing the test site. No cleaning up databases or running uninstall routines that leave cruft around if they don't complete successfully.

What You'll Need

One characteristic of the experienced craftsman is that he lays out his tools and determines what else he needs before he begins working. No running to the hardware store halfway through a job because he didn't have a 5/16 hex head wrench! Similarly, here I'll explain what you need in order to get started with DokuWiki - both in terms of hardware and software as well as knowledge and experience prerequisites.

Development Environment

First, let me describe what my development environment looks like. I've got quite a varied environment; while it is unlikely your environment is exactly like mine, there is very probably one machine laying around here that is similar to yours. And most hardcore developers love taking a peek over the shoulder of another developer to see how they've got their stuff set up.

I have three machines on my desk – all running various flavors of Linux and Windows in multi-boot scenarios, all are running the latest versions of Firefox and Chrome. Each machine is configured with a single data partition that all OSs point to. This data partition is mirrored across machines via the cloud (Dropbox). Thus the same data is accessible regardless of how the machine was booted, and the data is, obviously, organized in the same file structure regardless of what box it's on. In essence, every machine and OS is looking at the same data.

As mentioned in the previous chapter, I keep all my websites in a folder named Sites. This folder lies on the root level of the data partition.

Hentzenwerke Publishing, Inc.
books@hentzenwerke.com • www.hentzenwerke.com

The Web server software for each machine, be it Apache on Linux or IIS on Windows, points to the same place, the \Sites root. Thus, I can access specific sites like so:

```
http://localhost/dev_site_1
http://localhost/dev_site_2
```

regardless if I'm using Linux or Windows.

I'm going to assume that, during this discussion, you're using Windows. When we start discussing the installation of DokuWiki on the production server, we'll be using Linux.

Development Machine Requirements

In order to follow along on your development machine, you'll need two things:

1) A copy of DokuWiki on a Stick. This is the latest version of DokuWiki packaged with its own version of the Apache Web Server (microApache), configured so that it can be easily installed on Windows. It's called "on a Stick" because it's designed to be run from a thumb drive while you're trying DokuWiki out.

2) A reasonably modern browser. In general, all the latest versions of modern browsers, including Firefox, Chrome, Konqueror and Opera work fine. The wiki:compatibility page has a long list of browsers together with what works and what's broken, and how badly.

Download DokuWiki on a Stick

DokuWiki on a Stick comes as a compressed file that is assembled on the fly after you make a number of configuration settings on the download page. Let's do it together.

1. Navigate to download.dokuwiki.org.

2. In the center column, 'toggle all' to uncheck all languages unless you want to add additional languages. One of the many marvels of DokuWiki is the wide support of languages – dozens and dozens. This is done by including additional files for each language in the DokuWiki file structure. For example, in the "inc" folder is a "lang" folder which includes separate folders for each language checked. This construct is repeated throughout the DokuWiki file structure.

As a result, there can be a LOT of files in the DokuWiki file structure if you select a lot of languages. Only including the languages you explicitly want will greatly reduce the number of files included in installation.

3. Check the languages you want. English is always enabled.

4. In the left column, at the bottom, check Include Web-Server checkbox. This bundles the microApache Web Server in the zip file.

5. Click "Start download" button at the bottom of the left column.

6. After a few moments, the DokuWiki Creates page displays. It's pretty amazing, the resulting file has been created on the fly, including just the languages you selected, and whether or not you want the Web Server included.

7. Select where to save the resulting file. It'll be named something like this:

```
dokuwiki-460ee2279ccc3e08c706c287598b2298.tgz
```

The unusual (to Windows users) extension indicates that this is a zipped tar file. You may have to unzip twice, depending on which zip program you're using.

8. Unzip to a temp location. You'll get a folder named after the file, and within the folder, a second folder named DokiWikiStick, like so:

```
dokuwiki-460ee2279ccc3e08c706c287598b2298\DokuWikiStick
```

All of the files you need to run DokuWiki are in the DokuWikiStick folder; it's completely self-contained – even the Web Server. As a result, you can move the DokuWikiStick folder anywhere you want.

9. Move DokuWikiStick folder to where you'd like to keep it, maybe \dev or (where I put it) \sites. As an aside, I also rename the DokuWikiStick folder "DWS" since I do hate to type and thus abbreviate whenever I can.

Run DokuWiki on a Stick

In the DokuWikiStick root, there's a Windows script called run.cmd. This is simply a Windows Command Script – what old-timers call a 'batch file'.

Execute the script however you like, say, by double-clicking on it in your file manager. Depending on your Windows configuration, you may get a Windows Security Alert, as shown in **Figure 1**.

Figure 1. Windows Security Alert.

If you do get the Alert, check the Private checkbox and uncheck the Public checkbox, then click the Allow Access button.

A Windows Command box will display, like **Figure 2**.

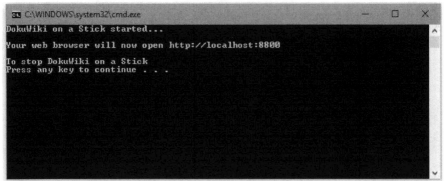

Figure 2. *Windows Command box running microApache.*

What you've just done is start the Web server. The script then looks for a file that indicates whether DokuWiki has been installed (local.php), and either starts DokuWiki for use, or runs the install script.

You'll need to keep the Command box open while you're working, but you can minimize it to get it out of the way. (Closing the command box will shut the Web server down.)

The DokuWiki Installer

The purpose of the DokuWiki installer is four-fold. First, it'll verify that all files and functions exist. Next, it'll ensure that file permissions have been set correctly. (These aren't applicable to DokuWiki on a Stick.) Third, it'll allow you to set a couple of initial configuration options. Finally, it'll (optionally) create an administrator account and an initial ACL ("Access Control List") policy.

The first time you run the run.cmd script, the install page will display. See **Figure 3**.

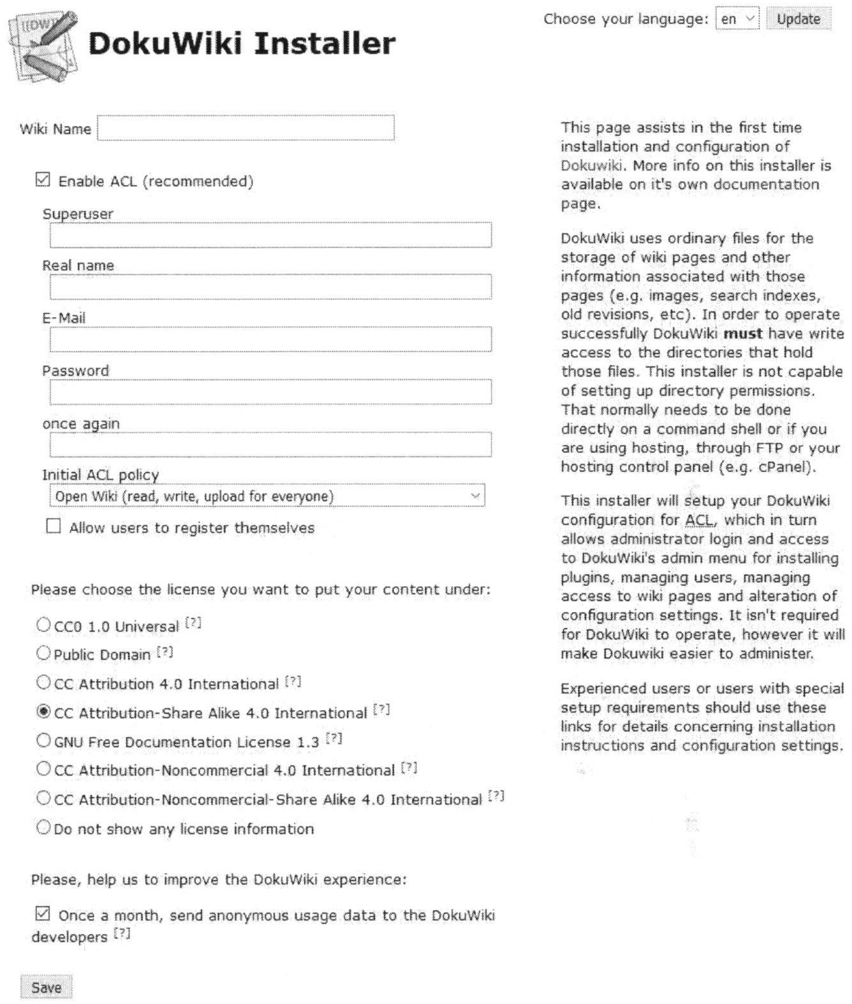

DokuWiki Installer

Choose your language: en ∨ Update

Wiki Name [_____]

☑ Enable ACL (recommended)

Superuser
[_____]

Real name
[_____]

E-Mail
[_____]

Password
[_____]

once again
[_____]

Initial ACL policy
[Open Wiki (read, write, upload for everyone)   ∨]

☐ Allow users to register themselves

Please choose the license you want to put your content under:

○ CC0 1.0 Universal [?]
○ Public Domain [?]
○ CC Attribution 4.0 International [?]
◉ CC Attribution-Share Alike 4.0 International [?]
○ GNU Free Documentation License 1.3 [?]
○ CC Attribution-Noncommercial 4.0 International [?]
○ CC Attribution-Noncommercial-Share Alike 4.0 International [?]
○ Do not show any license information

Please, help us to improve the DokuWiki experience:

☑ Once a month, send anonymous usage data to the DokuWiki developers [?]

[Save]

This page assists in the first time installation and configuration of DokuWiki. More info on this installer is available on it's own documentation page.

DokuWiki uses ordinary files for the storage of wiki pages and other information associated with those pages (e.g. images, search indexes, old revisions, etc). In order to operate successfully DokuWiki **must** have write access to the directories that hold those files. This installer is not capable of setting up directory permissions. That normally needs to be done directly on a command shell or if you are using hosting, through FTP or your hosting control panel (e.g. cPanel).

This installer will setup your DokuWiki configuration for ACL, which in turn allows administrator login and access to DokuWiki's admin menu for installing plugins, managing users, managing access to wiki pages and alteration of configuration settings. It isn't required for DokuWiki to operate, however it will make Dokuwiki easier to administer.

Experienced users or users with special setup requirements should use these links for details concerning installation instructions and configuration settings.

***Figure 3**. Initial empty installation page.*

Let's walk through each item on the page. In Chapter 6, I'll explain each of the permutations of the other available options.

Choose your language combo box: First, easy to miss - the combo box in the upper right corner defines what language messages and prompts will be displayed in the wiki. By default, it's set to English, but if you open the combo, you'll see a list of all of the language options you selected in Step 3 in the previous section.

Wiki Name text box: The name will show up in the top banner of every wiki page (see **Figure 7**), so choose it with some thought. You can change it later, but still, an off-the-cuff shot like "Some Dorki Wiki" is probably not the best choice.

Enable ACL (recommended) checkbox: The "Enable ACL (recommended)" checkbox is checked by default (thus the 'recommended' admonition.) ACL stands for "Access Control Lists" and they are just what they sound like - lists that control access to the wiki. Since we're interested in creating a private wiki just for our software development group, we'll need ACLs enabled. Keep it checked.

Superuser textbox: Enter a username for the administrator. This will typically be you. Note that the name of the user (and Full name, next option) who is logged in displays at the top right of the page (**Figure 8**), and the name of the user who edits a page is displayed at the bottom of the page (**Figure 12**) as well as in the page history, so choose your superuser name with care as well. Slang or off-color names may appear funny now but they'll come back to haunt you - and they're a huge pain to fix.

Full name textbox: The value you enter here is used in Email notifications and RSS feeds as well as displayed in the upper right of pages.

Email textbox: The value you enter here is the address used when you request to have password sent to you ("password reset") and if you choose to be notified via email when pages are modified (namespace and page subscriptions.)

Password and **once again** textboxes: Passwords are.... passwords. They're encrypted in the system. The type of encryption can be changed in the configuration later on.

Initial ACL Policy combo box: Finally, the "Initial ACL policy" combo box determines how non-admin users will be able to access pages. Select "Closed wiki" since this is a private wiki.

Allow users to register themselves checkbox: If checked, any visitor can register themselves, which then allows them full access to the wiki.

License option group: Up to you, use the question mark links to educate yourself about the differences.

Send anonymous usage data checkbox: As explained on the Web page itself. When done filling in the values, the resulting form should look like **Figure 4**.

DokuWiki Installer

Choose your lar

Wiki Name | Dynamite Construction Machines

☑ Enable ACL (recommended)

Superuser
| whil |

Real name
| Whil Hentzen |

E-Mail
| whil@whilhentzen.com |

Password
| •••••••• |

once again
| •••••••• |

Initial ACL policy
| Closed Wiki (read, write, upload for registered users only)   ∨ |

☐ Allow users to register themselves

Th
ins
Do
is ;
do

Do
stc
inf
pa
olc
op
ha
th;
no
pe
be
or
FT
(e.

Th
Do

Figure 4. *The DokuWiki Installer page, filled in.*

Once you've filled in the fields, click the Save button at the bottom of the page, and you should be greeted with a confirmation page as shown in **Figure 5**.

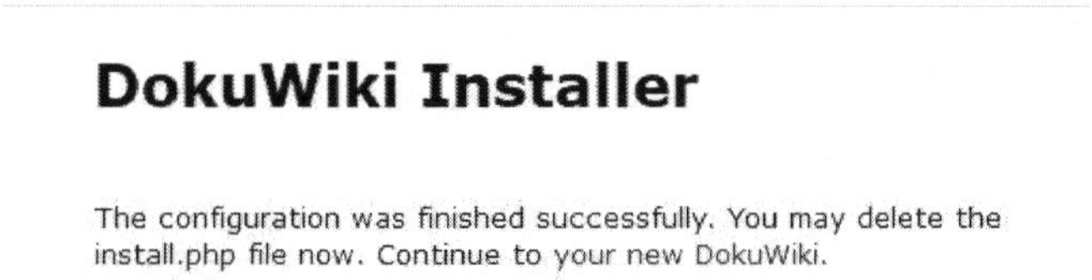

DokuWiki Installer

The configuration was finished successfully. You may delete the install.php file now. Continue to your new DokuWiki.

Figure 5. *Confirmation of a successful install.*

In the DWS folder there are two subfolders, dokuwiki and server. In the root of the dokuwiki folder, there's a file named 'install.php' which you **should** delete. Not doing so allows anyone else to navigate to your wiki, passing 'install.php' as a parameter, and rerun the installation.

The link that says "to your new DokuWiki" will take you to the home page of your brand new wiki. (***Don't click it yet!***) Which home page will depend on which Initial ACL Policy you chose. If you selected "Closed Wiki", the home page will be a login page. See **Figure 6**.

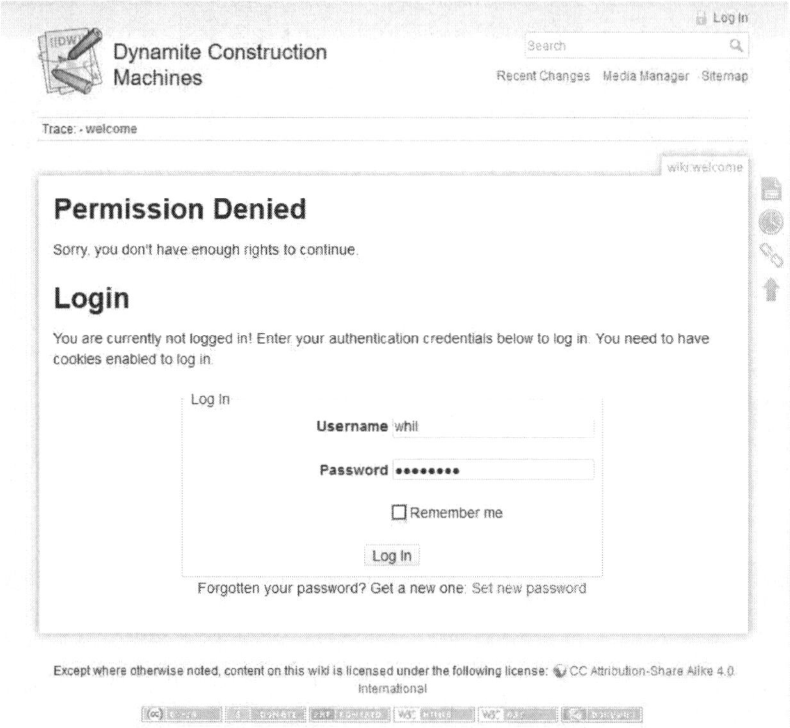

Figure 6. *The login page.*

However, ***before you click*** that and we get going, it'd be handy to know how to get to your wiki without using this link, since you probably won't ever see this page again.

Start DokuWiki From Now On

In the future, you can again run the run.cmd script, and since installation has been run, the login page will be displayed. You're now ready to get to work - with a start page that contains no content. Chapter 5 provides a brief description of the contents of the wiki page and how to create, edit and save a basic "Hello World" page.

Under the Hood

At this point, let's take a look at what's been installed. We've got a DWS folder on your development drive somewhere (say, under \Sites.) Under DWS there are two folders, dokuwiki and server, and the run.cmd file.

The first folder, dokuwiki, contains the dokuwiki software and has a place for data dokuwiki\data. The folder dokuwiki\data\pages contains the files that populate the actual wiki Web pages.

The server folder, obviously, contains the microApache Web server. When you install dokuwiki on a Web server, only the dokuwiki folder will be created.

What's Next?

Logging in for the first time displays the DokuWiki Welcome page, as shown in **Figure 7**. We'll pick up here in Chapter 5.

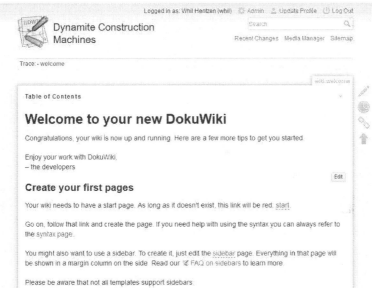

Figure 7. The DokuWiki Welcome page.

Now let's finish the process.

First, close your browser. (If you just close that tab, authentication will likely stick around.) Then, in the Windows Command Box (back in Figure 2), press any key and the web server shuts down and the Command Box goes away.

Conclusion

I've covered the basic steps to your first DokuWiki installation on a development machine. In the next chapters, I'll explore the various installations options in detail.

Hentzenwerke Publishing, Inc.
books@hentzenwerke.com • www.hentzenwerke.com

4: Linux Server Quick Install

Now it's time to install DokuWiki in production - on your Linux Web Server.

A wiki doesn't do much good if its only on your own machine. Its so much more useful on a publicly facing web server. DokuWiki has been around for a long time, and it's now available in the 'one click' installs on many Web hosts. If so, you pretty much don't need to read this chapter.

If, however, your particular hosting environment doesn't include DokuWiki, here's the quick How To for you. In this chapter, I'll describe the basics on how to install DokuWiki on a Linux Web server.

I assume that you've got a website, and thus access to your Web server. If you don't, then maybe it's time to consider it. I mean, you want to have a wiki, you're going to need a web site, right?

And I'm going to further assume that your wiki will be hosted in a folder under the root of your web site's folder structure. With that, let's begin.

What You'll Need

One of the best parts of DokuWiki (and there are lots of them!) is the install process if you're doing it yourself. After reading through this chapter a couple of times, if you can't install a new DokuWiki wiki and have it ready for testing in five minutes, you're just not paying attention.

Installation onto a machine consists of eight painless steps. The first three: prepare a location on your machine, make sure your Web server is running and make sure it's capable of running PHP. (The last five, covered in the next section, are to download, extract, copy, install, and run.) The installation topic on the DokuWiki wiki inserts another step in this process - handling security. I do basic security set up here, but not in detail, because we'll deal with security in great detail soon enough, and it isn't critical to dive in with both feet now on a test install that you're going to blow away.

Server Requirements

1. First, your Web server has to support PHP. Apache and PHP go together like, well, any two things that go together really really well. Visit www.apache.org, for more information. I know, it's kind of hard to believe that I have to explicitly say this, but better to be safe than assume.

2. Second, check that the most recent PHP supported by your host is installed on the server. The wiki's page, install:php, has a number of notes about specific PHP configuration items. Additionally, cruise by www.php.org, for more information on PHP configuration in general.

3. And, third, again, a reasonably modern browser. As mentioned in the previous chapter, all of the latest versions of browsers work pretty well. It seems that I

shouldn't have to say this but every once in a while I run across someone who is still insisting on using Netscape 2 or Lynx, insisting that it works fine for them.

Unlike installation mechanisms for other wikis, as long as you have access to an FTP client or a file manager where you are going to put your DokuWiki files, you'll be fine. You don't have to run scripts or batch files or otherwise have root access. You may have to change permissions on some folders, but most shared hosts provide a mechanism to do so. If yours doesn't provide that minimal functionality, perhaps it's time to find a new Web host.

Prep the Landing Spot for your Wiki

Let's lay some groundwork before we jump into installation. To wit, let's prepare a place for our wiki before we start installation.

While technically you could install DokuWiki in the root of your server's folder structure, what happens when you want a second wiki? Because like the commercial said, you can't just have one. Web sites, that is. So I point my Web server root to the top level folder, add folders beneath the top level for each wiki, and then access a specific site by including that folder's name. On a local box, these URLs would look like this:

```
http://localhost/Hentzenwerke
http://localhost/WhilHentzen/cust_one
```

And the production server URLs look like this:

```
http://www.hentzenwerke.com
http://www.WhilHentzen.com/cust_one
```

The Web server will look for the default page in that directory. Taking the suggestion of having a custom "index.html" file one step, further, consider having a distinctive landing page for each wiki so it's easy to tell where you are. Having the same generic Hello World page as the default page for every wiki won't be very helpful when troubleshooting.

All this said, we're not going to download and install the files direct to your server. Instead, we'll download to your local machine, unpack and then FTP up to your server.

Make Sure your Web Server is Running

Technically, this step is more important when you're setting up a new box; it shouldn't be needed on a server that's already dishing out a web site.

Verify PHP is Installed and Running

This one is more demanding. Just because PHP is theoretically installed on your Web server, you can't simply assume that it's working. In order to test, you could (and should) create a simple PHP page (named index.php) that you can use to make sure that PHP is installed and running. I have a test PHP page (index.php, found on www.hentzenwerke.com under this book's downloads) in the root with the following contents:

```
<html>
<head>
<title>Root folder, now displayed in living color, via PHP: Hello
World</title>
</head>
</body>
<h1>Hello World</h1>
<?php echo "Golly, I'm a PHP script (index.php) running on the root
page.";
?>
<br><br>
<?php
echo('Today is... ' . date('l, F Y. ') );
?>
<br><br>
<?php
phpinfo()
?>
</body>
</html>
```

Running this page via http://<your domain>/index.php will display a page like shown in **Figure 1**.

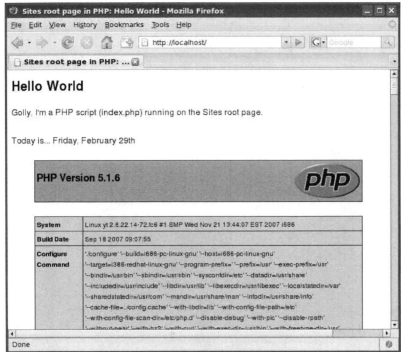

Figure 1. *Localhost serving up the default PHP file.*

(I ran this on localhost on my dev box because I'm not overly fond of displaying server information in public.)

This is a great tool to verify that PHP is installed and running properly. (A significant percentage of DokuWiki installation problems end up being a result of an incorrect PHP installation.) Note that the PHP code tells you both the current date and time, and lists the configuration of your PHP installation, which is very handy for troubleshooting. I recommend you do this if you haven't already.

As a Best Practice, it's good to have a script with phpinfo() available when you're troubleshooting, but you don't want to leave that script on a page accessible by the outside world, as it will tell the Bad Guys too much about how your site is configured, and thus, give them information that would be useful in hacking your site.

Installing DokuWiki on a Server

Now we get to the last five steps - download, extract, copy, install, and run.

Download

To download, navigate to

```
http://www.dokuwiki.org
```

The resulting page looks something like Figure 2.

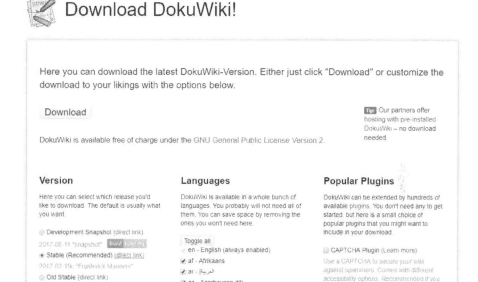

Figure 2. *The DokuWiki download page.*

Click the Toggle All button to remove all of the language packs (except English) and then check any that you'd like to include. Click on the green "Download" button in the center of the page. The link for the current version, options to customize it with languages and plugins, as well as the current version under development and older releases are all available on this page.

The latest release is found in the link next to the "Stable (Recommended)" label on the left side of the page. Clicking "direct link" will download a file named

```
dokuwiki-stable.tgz
```

If you're a Windows developer, the 'tgz' extension may unnerve you a bit. Not to worry - it's simply a ZIP file produced by a Linux archiving program. Most popular Windows compression programs will be able to handle this file without pause. The details are on the install:unpacking page on the DokuWiki site.

Download the file and pop it somewhere on your drive where you want to work with it. I have a folder on my local machine called "zips" which is where all my downloaded files land. Once I decide a file is worth keeping, I send a copy off to an archive folder on my file server so if I need it again, I don't have to rely on being able to connect to the Web site that was hosting the original.

In this case, however, I immediately put the dokuwiki-stable.tgz file in the dw_masters folder (described earlier in the "DokuWiki files location" section) so that I can begin working with it.

Extract Files

Once downloaded, the next step is to unzip the file. Depending on what software and mechanism you use, you will eventually end up with a folder named 'dokuwiki-cccc-mm-dd' (where cccc-mm-dd represents the date of the build, such as 2017-02-19), with the following contents:

```
/bin
/conf
/data
/inc
/lib
.htaccess.dist
COPYING
doku.php
feed.php
index.php
install.php
README
VERSION
```

(You're safe using an "Extract here" menu option from your file extraction software, as opposed to 'Extract to dokuwiki-stable' because the files in the .tgz file are already wrapped in a dokuwiki-cccc-mm-dd folder. 'Extract here' will create the dokuwiki... folder for you.)

A view of this structure is shown in **Figure 3**.

Name ▲	Ext	Size	Type	Modified	Attr
bin			File Folder	Friday 09:32	-a---
conf			File Folder	Friday 09:32	-a---
data			File Folder	Friday 09:32	-a---
inc			File Folder	Friday 09:32	-----
lib			File Folder	Friday 09:32	-a---
vendor			File Folder	Friday 09:32	-a---
.htaccess.dist	dist	1,744	DIST File	Friday 09:32	-a---
COPYING		18,092	File	Friday 09:32	-a---
doku.php	php	3,692	PHP File	Friday 09:32	-a---
feed.php	php	19,374	PHP File	Friday 09:32	-a---
index.php	php	2,097	PHP File	Friday 09:32	-a---
install.php	php	20,700	PHP File	Friday 09:32	-a---
README		306	File	Friday 09:32	-a---
VERSION		33	File	Friday 09:32	-a---

F:\Dropbox\Sites\dw_masters\dokuwiki-2017-02-19c

Figure 3. *The Dokuwiki folder structure.*

This looks like a lot of stuff all of a sudden, but I'll explain it all in short order. Right now, let's look at the contents of the dokuwiki-cccc-mm-dd folder.

The index.php and install.php files are the main programs that we'll need. Thus, you can see that the dokuwiki-cccc-mm-dd folder represents the root of the DokuWiki file system.

There should be maybe 1000 files scattered among dozens of folders. If you didn't uncheck all of the localizations earlier, you'll find that there are around 4200 files scattered among 740 folders. The difference are internationalization files for DokuWiki. The core engine has been translated into nearly 70 languages, each of which has its own set of folders for a variety of purposes. Additional components have also been translated into a number of languages, each of which also requires a bucketful of files. The default dokuwiki-stable.tgz file contains all languages, thus the multitude of files.

Copy to Destination

We're simply going to copy the entire dokuwiki-cccc-mm-dd folder structure to our Web server folder, and then rename the dokuwiki-cccc-mm-dd folder to a name more to our liking. For example, suppose I want to create a wiki for 'cust_one' on my 'whilhentzen.com' Web site. I'll copy the DokuWiki folder so it lands here:

```
/Sites/whilhentzen/dokuwiki-cccc-mm-dd
```

and then I'll rename it, like so:

```
/Sites/whilhentzen/cust_one
```

I'll FTP that folder to my Web host's cust_one folder, and navigate to it with my browser like so:

```
http://www.whilhentzen.com/cust_one
```

When I create a second wiki for another customer, I'll copy the DokuWiki folder again, and then rename it so the wiki files end up in

```
/Sites/whilhentzen/cust_two
```

I'll FTP that folder to my Web host's cust_two folder, and navigate to that wiki with my browser like so:

```
http://www.whilhentzen.com/cust_two
```

(You may be asking yourself if this means that each wiki is using its own copy of the software, and the answer is yes. This is not a concern because the entire system (without your content) only comprises a couple of megabytes (about 7 MB if you keep all of the internationalization files) and it's extremely easy to update the source code to a newer version. Additionally, there's a technique that allows you to use one set of DokuWiki code to run multiple, separate wikis, described at **tips:farm**.

Up to this point, I've used generic examples of 'cust_one' and 'cust_two' for names of wikis. From now on, I'll use a more palatable example - a wiki for the specification of a software program that allows sales reps of my favorite customer, "Dynamite Construction Machines", to develop customized configurations of their products for their customers.

Run the installer

As I mentioned earlier, there are two files of immediate interest in the DokuWiki root: index.php and install.php. These are text files that contain PHP programs. You navigate to them in your browser just like an HTML page. The Apache Web server, if properly configured, will take the PHP code in a PHP program (or 'script', as they are more commonly referred to), interpret it, and return results.

We're most interested in "install.php" at the moment. To execute it, enter

```
http://<comain>/path-to-dokuwiki/install.php
```

in your browser. For me, this URL is

```
http://www.whilhentzen.com/dcm/install.php
```

The Apache Web server will execute the program and return the result - the DokuWiki Installer Web page, as shown in **Figure 4**.

Figure 4. The Dokuwiki Installer page.

The fields on this page have been discussed in Section 3, DokuWiki Installer, so I won't repeat that information. Again. When done filling in the values, the resulting form should look like **Figure 5**.

DokuWiki Installer

Choose your lar

Wiki Name Dynamite Construction Machines

☑ Enable ACL (recommended)

Superuser

whil

Real name

Whil Hentzen

E-Mail

whil@whilhentzen.com

Password

••••••••

once again

••••••••

Initial ACL policy

Closed Wiki (read, write, upload for registered users only) ⌄

☐ Allow users to register themselves

Th
ins
Do
is :
do

Do
st(
inf
pa
olc
op
ha
tha
no
pe
be
or
FT
(e.

Th
Do

Figure 5. *The DokuWiki Installer page, filled in.*

Once you've filled in the fields, click the Save button at the bottom of the page, and you should be greeted with a confirmation page as shown in **Figure 6**.

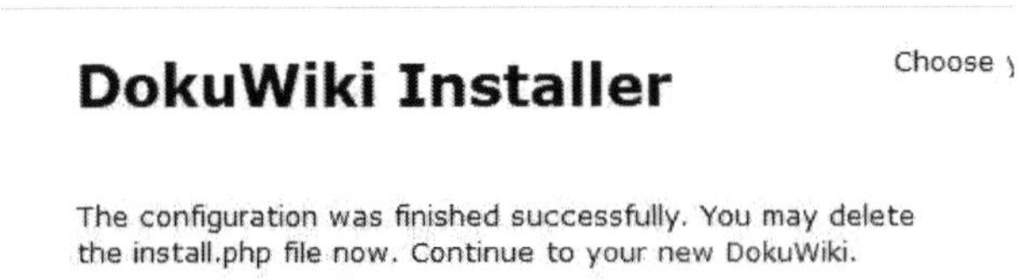

DokuWiki Installer

Choose)

The configuration was finished successfully. You may delete
the install.php file now. Continue to your new DokuWiki.

Figure 6. *Confirmation of a successful install.*

Click on the 'to your new DokuWiki' link and you'll see the login page, as shown in **Figure 7**.

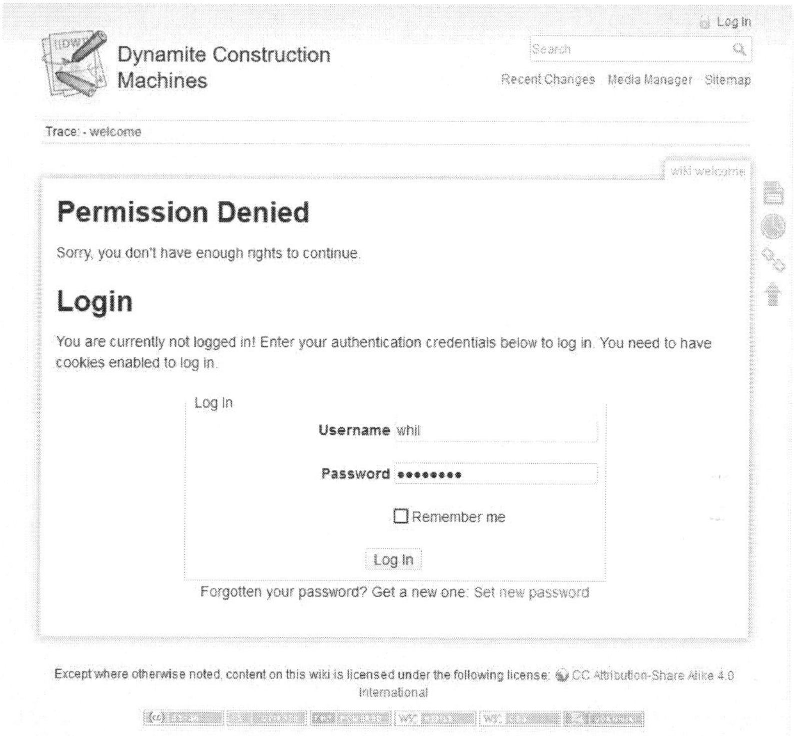

Figure 7. The login page.

However, before you click that and we get going, it'd be handy to know how to get to your wiki without using this link, since you probably won't ever see this page again.

Start DokuWiki From Now On

Now that the wiki has been created and you've logged in, you can just run the index.php program to load the wiki from now on, like so:

```
http://<domain>/path-to-dokuwiki/index.php
```

For me, this is

```
http://www.whilhentzen.com/dcm/index.php
```

Actually, if you've configured Apache to recognize index.php as a default home page, you can just enter the directory and index.php will be executed automatically:

```
http://www.whilhentzen.com/dcm
```

What's Next?

Logging in for the first time displays the DokuWiki Welcome page, as shown in **Figure 8**. We'll pick up here in Chapter 5.

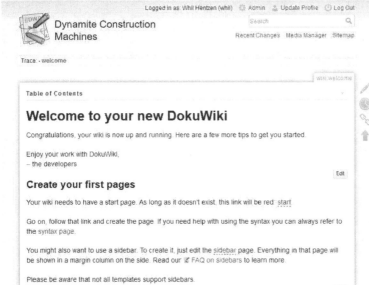

Figure 8. The DokuWiki Welcome page.

Problems

During installation, it's possible that you've run into a problem. The most common problem displays a page that looks like **Figure 9**.

Figure 9. The manifestation of a common installation problem.

Whoa. Let's take a look at what's going on here. At this point, some folks run into file permission problems, both locally and when installing it on a shared host. In short, the /data and /conf folders - and all of the subfolders in /data (there aren't any subfolders in /conf) - must be writable by the Web server user in order to work. After all, the Web server will be writing to all of those folders.

Given the wide variety of possible configurations, it's dangerous to try to provide a single fix-all command. There are a number of very useful topics on the DokuWiki wiki. There's an excellent, excellent, excellent screencast that discusses how to install on a hosted server, and it covers permission problems in some detail. Additionally, the **install:permissions** help topic has further info about handling permissions. I suggest you read through the topic several times in addition to the discussion in this book.

5: Working with a Wiki Page

Now that we have a working wiki, we should work with it. More specifically, let's look at how to create, edit, and save a page, and then see what's going on under the hood.

Before we create a page, we should see what we've got to work with. Log in as discussed in both Chapters 3 and 4, and you'll be greeted with the DokuWiki Welcome page, repeated again here in **Figure 1**.

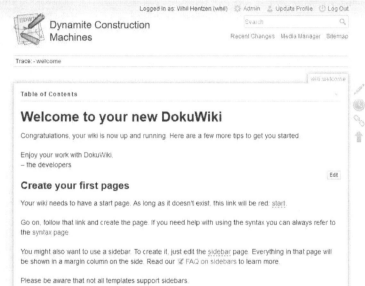

Figure 1. The DokuWiki Welcome page.

Starting from the upper left, here's what you see.

[[DW]] logo
This is the default logo for all DokuWikis. You can change it later; discussed in Chapter 6.

Dynamite Construction Machines label
This is the title of the site, entered during installation. This can be changed using the Configuration Manager. The title of the site is also a hyperlink that points back to the main page of the wiki. See **Figure 2**.

Figure 2. *Wiki name.*

Logged in as row

The Full Name and username of the logged in user are displayed in the upper left. Next to those values are links for Admin (superusers only), Update Profile, and Log Out. See **Figure 3**.

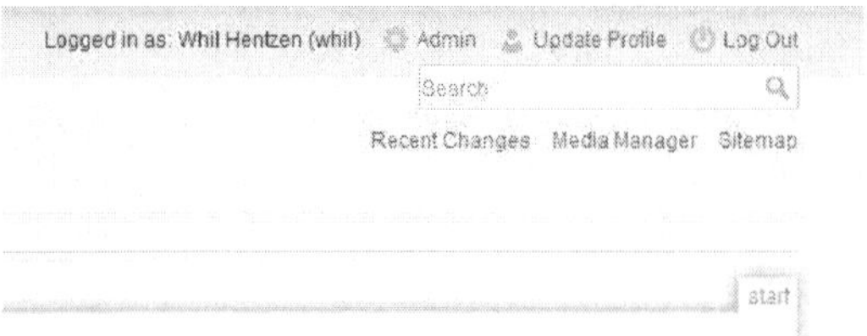

Figure 3. *Wiki logged in user information.*

Search Textbox and Button

Entering a word or phrase will generate two lists of matching results. The first is a list of page names that match contain the search term. The second is a list of pages where the search term was found in the contents of the page, together with the number of times the term was found in the page.

Recent Changes button

Clicking this button will display a list of up to the 20 most recently changed pages in the wiki. (Note: the listed changes are for the entire wiki, not just the current page.) If there are more than 20 pages that have been changed, a "less recent >>" button will display under the list. See Chapter 10 for a detailed explanation of how this works.

Media Manager link

The Media Manager is the page where you can upload files, including graphics, documents, screen shots, and archives, to embed in the wiki.

Sitemap link

The sitempa is an automatically generated list of all the topics in the wiki.

Trace: start label

The light grey band under the row of buttons, with the word "Trace:" aligned to the left will display your history of navigation through the wiki, much like a browser history (a.k.a. breadcrumbs). Settings in the Configuration Manager control how many levels will be shown or allow the band to be turned off completely.

Edit box

The meat of the wiki is the box under the Trace label. Normally it's a read-only box; when the page is being edited, it'll turn into a resizable editbox. The name of the page is in the tab in the upper right corner.

Right-aligned Toolbar buttons

The four buttons to the right of the box provide a variety of page-related functionality. This toolbar floats along the browser viewport as you scroll the page.

Edit this page/Create this page button

The top button provides either an Add or Edit functionality. Before the page is created, the button will display a pencil and a (+) sign, with a "Create this page" the tooltip. Once the page is created, the (+) sign disappears and the tooltip changes to "Edit this page". When editing, the button changes to "Show Page." The next section will cover this process.

Old revisions button

Once a page has been edited, old versions of the page - previous copies of this page that were saved - are stored and available for viewing via the "Old revisions" button. Clicking the button will display a list of older versions; clicking on an entry in the list will display that page. See Chapter 6 for a detailed explanation of how this works.

Backlinks

Backlinks list all of the topics that have links to the page you're viewing.

Back to Top

A page has no pre-defined length. As a result, it can become quite long, and it's a nuisance to scroll back to the top. Clicking this button scrolls to the very top of the page.

Last Modified labels

Just below the area showing the content of the page, there's a label showing the name of the file containing the text for this page as well as the date, time and user who last modified the page.

License

The license you choose for the wiki is displayed. This can be updated in the configuration page.

Footer images

The 5 images at the bottom of the page identify various attributes about the wiki and provide additional functions, such as creating an RSS feed, donating to the DokuWiki author and links to the W3C, CSS and DokuWiki Web sites.

Now that we know our way around, let's do something.

Login button

If you enable ACLs and select "Open wiki" in the Initial ACL Policy combo, you'll see a Login button displayed. Clicking this button will display a login page. Since this was configured as an open wiki, you may think that the Login button is unnecessary. When ACLs are enabled on an open wiki, the Login restricts access to the Administration functions to the superuser who was identified during installation.

Create and Save a Page

Now that we know our way around, let's create and save a page.

As the Welcome page says, your wiki needs to have a start page (what we used to call a 'home page' in the olden days.) This will be the page all users see every time they open the wiki, so it's the perfect place for introductory information for new users, links to frequently referenced pages and anything else you find useful. Much like the Welcome page that DokuWiki displays upon installation.

To create the start page, click on the red 'start' link with dashed underlines. (The red and dashed underlines are visual clues that the page doesn't exist but the word is intended to be a link.)

Once you click on the red 'start' link, you'll be greeted with a 'This topic does not exist' page, both a notification that the page doesn't exist as well as a placeholder for creating a new page. See **Figure 9**.

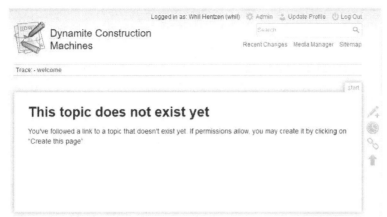

Figure 9.Start page creation.

"This topic does not exist yet"

Now we come to the interesting part of the page - the page header and the contents of the page. I'll address the basic process of creating a page in the next section; Chapter 9 covers the creation and editing of a page in detail.

Float your mouse over the toolbox to the right of the text area, and you'll see the toolbar expands to include text such as "Create this page" next to the icons. Click the top icon on the right toolbar, the pencil with a (+) sign next to it, the 'Add' mechanism. After clicking, you'll be redirected to a new page, and you'll be greeted with a blank page with an edit box, formatting icons above the box and Save, Preview and Cancel buttons below. See **Figure 10**.

Figure 10. *Editing the Start page.*

I'll go into much greater detail on how to use all the gizmos on this page in Chapter 9. For the time being, just type some text into the edit box as I did in Figure 10, and then click the Save button at the bottom. The results are shown in **Figure 11** - a brand new wiki page - your first!

Figure 11*. Start page saved.*

You'll also see your username in the lower right under the box, along with the name of the test file that contains the page you just created and the timestamp. See **Figure 12**.

start.txt · Last modified: 2017/08/12 01:43 by whil

Figure 12*. Start page last modified data.*

Under the Hood
Oh, and since you're a programmer, you probably want to know what's happened behind the scenes. There's now a new text file called "start.txt" in the DWS/dokuwiki/data/pages folder under your DokuWiki installation. You can open this file with any text editor and view the contents.

6. Quick Customizations

Nothing better than to make your wiki your own from the very beginning. Here are three quick tweaks you can make to make your visitors feel at home.

Three things your visitors will want to do. The first is to make sure they're at the right place. The second is to give them a quick tour of the site, a quick start, instructions to get rolling. And the third is to give them an easy mechanism to navigate the site.

Before we get into the heavy lifting of documenting the New New Thing in Software.

Customize the Logo

Up to this point, you've seen the default DokuWiki logo in the upper left hand corner. Wouldn't it be great to see your own logo there? The folks at Dynamite Construction Machines spent thousands of hours and millions of dollars to create their logo, and they'd like to see it on their wiki.

Simple enough. The logo file is located here:

```
lib\tpl\dokuwiki\images\logo.png
```

Create your own logo and replace the existing logo.png file with your own. I'd suggest to make a back up of the original logo file as well as your own, just in case a future update or user error overwrites your custom file.

Once you've done that, refresh the page, and you'll see something like shown in **Figure 1**.

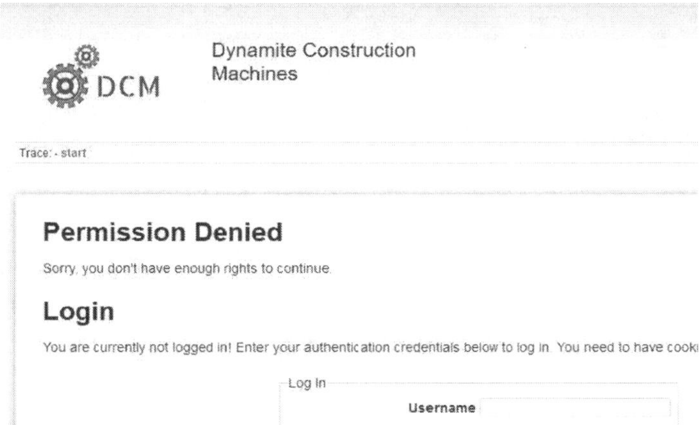

Figure 1. The million dollar DCM logo.

That million dollars was well spent, wasn't it? Now when visitors hit the wiki, they'll know they're at the right place.

The **template:dokuwiki** page provides additional detail on how to customize the logo, favicon, and bookmark icons.

Start Page

You've just created a start page in the previous chapter. Let's make it useful, because it will be the first thing that every visitor sees. Obviously the information you provide will depend on your visitor base, but there are a few things that are pretty common.

For example, a welcome message, instructions on using the sidebar and a reminder on how to create a new page, and perhaps links to some wiki references. An example is shown in **Figure 2**.

Figure 2. *Sample Start page with help visitor information.*

When DokuWiki is installed, a few help files are installed in the data\pages\wiki folder. I find it helpful to provide links to two of those pages, like so:

```
[[wiki:dokuwiki|DokuWiki information]]
[[wiki:syntax|DokuWiki Syntax]]
```

Additionally, I find it helpful to provide a link to the section on the Syntax page that identifies the characters that are automatically converted to display emoticons.

```
[[wiki:syntax#text_to_image_conversions|Smileys]]
```

You can find the images for the emoticons in dokuwiki\lib\images\smileys.

Install a Sidebar for Navigation

A wiki isn't much use without pages, but once you get past about three of them, it's kind of hard to keep track of them. It's trivially easy to add a sidebar to the wiki, a list of topics on the side that serve to navigate sections and individual pages so visitors can find things easily.

A sidebar is simply a standard wiki page that you flag as a sidebar, sort of like autoexec.bat and config.sys are text files that operating systems know to look for to do special things with. I've created a simple sidebar in **Figure 3** so that you can see where we're headed.

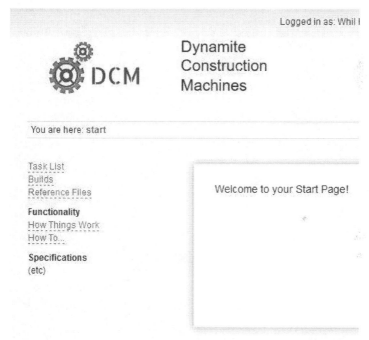

Figure 3. A sample side bar for navigation.

(The links are all dashed underlined because they haven't been created yet – this is a sample!)

Now, to get started, click on the Admin link in the upper right corner of the wiki page. (If there is no Admin link, it means whoever logged in isn't set up as an administrator, and that's a truly curious situation, as at this point you should be the only user and hence, by default, an administrator.)

Clicking on aforementioned Admin link brings forward the Administration page, shown in **Figure 4**.

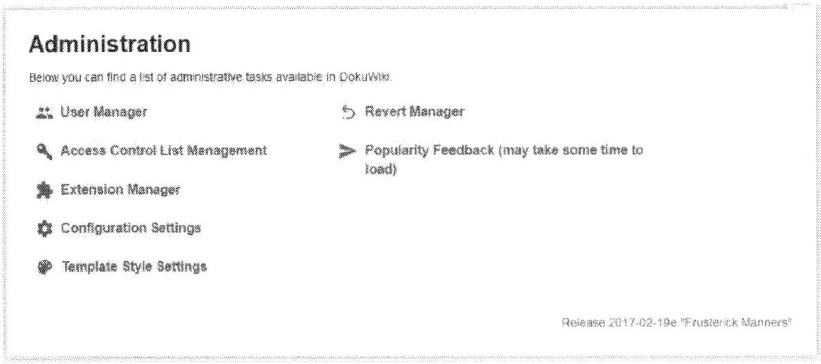

Figure 4. The Administration page.

Clicking on the Configuration Settings link on the left side brings forward the Configuration page, shown in **Figure 5**.

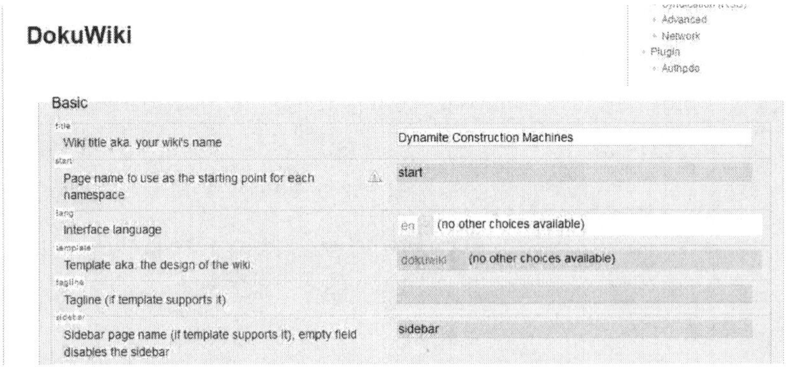

Figure 5. The top few settings in the Configuration page.

The Configuration page is long, very long, and that's why I've dedicated a full chapter to it. For the time being, though, we're just going to look at one setting- the name of the sidebar page.

The sixth setting down in the "Basic" sections is where you define the name of the page that will hold the contents of the sidebar. If you don't want a sidebar, you can do one of two things – either delete the value in this setting, or not create a wiki page with that name. As you can see, the default page name for the sidebar is 'sidebar', but since there's no 'sidebar.txt' file in the pages folder, there's no sidebar on the wiki.

Let's remedy that.

Leave the Configuration page, most easily by clicking on the DCM logo. Then, with your Start page displayed, click the pencil icon on the left in order to put the page into editing mode. You did this in Chapter 5, so you're an old pro by now.

Now that you're in editing mode, on a brand new blank line, enter the string

```
[[sidebar]]
```

as shown in **Figure 6**.

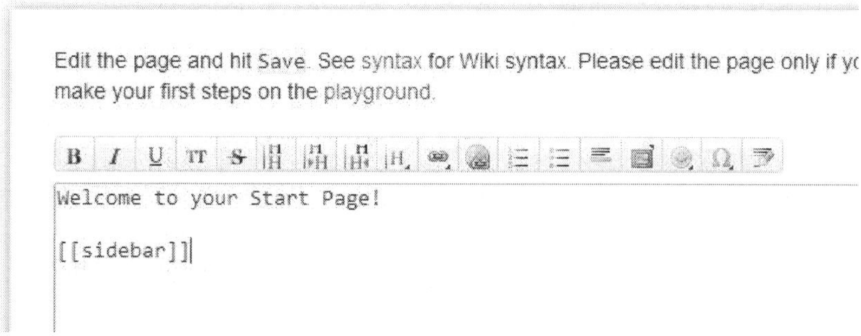

Figure 6. Entering a link to the sidebar page.

The double square brackets are code for "The word or phrase inside is the name of a wiki page to be created." Once you save the page, you'll get a link to a 'to be created' page as shown in **Figure 7**.

Trace: - sidebar - start

Welcome to your Start Page!

sidebar

Figure 7. A link to be your soon to be created sidebar page.

Click on the link and you'll get a "Dude! This page doesn't exist yet. Do you want to create it now?" message as shown in **Figure 8**.

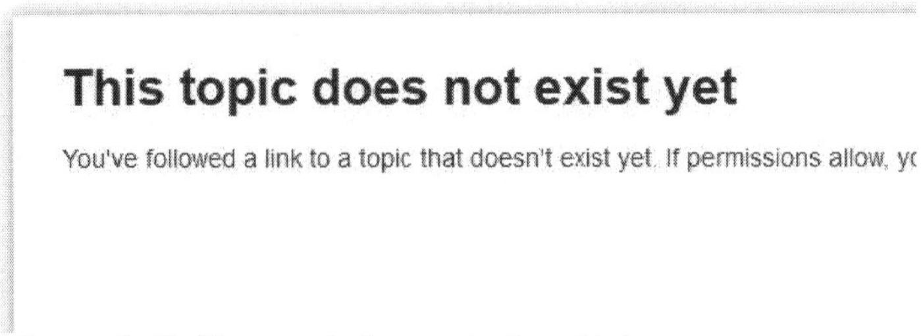

This topic does not exist yet

You've followed a link to a topic that doesn't exist yet. If permissions allow, yc

Figure 8. Getting ready to create the sidebar page.

Click on the pencil (+) icon on the right to create an empty page. This page will contain the content of the sidebar. Enter the link for a "Builds" page, as shown in **Figure 9**.

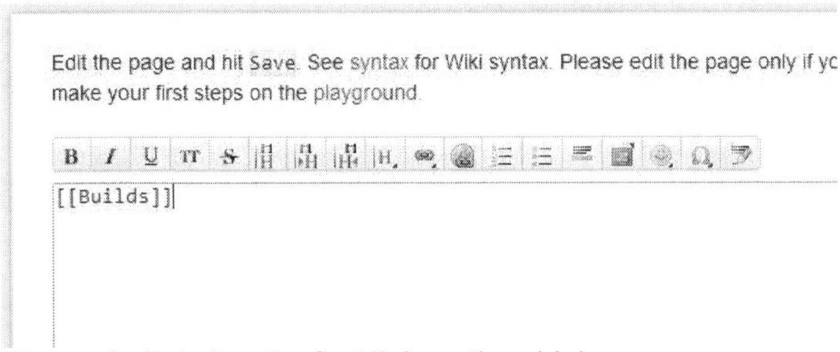

Edit the page and hit Save. See syntax for Wiki syntax. Please edit the page only if yc make your first steps on the playground.

```
[[Builds]]
```

Figure 9. Entering the first link on the sidebar page.

Upon saving the page with the Save button at the bottom, you'll get both a brand new sidebar as well as the display of the sidebar page in the main page window, as shown in **Figure 10**.

Trace: · start · sidebar

Builds

Builds

Figure 10. Your brand new sidebar, complete with the first link.

This may be disconcerting at first, it seems awkward that you see the sidebar appear on the left, but the box on the right also shows the text, because you're editing the page that contains the sidebar text. Click the logo again to get back to your Start page, and you'll be able to see what your new sidebar-adorned wiki looks like. Check out **Figure 11**.

Figure 11. Your wiki with the new sidebar.

You may notice that the sidebar is pretty big – it's not a coincidence that I accidentally typed 'widebar' twice. You can change the width via a configuration setting in the Template page. Click on the Admin link at the top of the page and then the Template Styles Settings link in the Administration page (Figure 4, back a bit) to open the Template Style Settings page as shown in **Figure 12**.

Template Style Settings

This tool allows you to change certain style settings of your currently selected template. All changes a
are upgrade safe.

Open as a popup

Main text color	#333333
Main background color	#ffffff
Alternative text color	#999999
Alternative background color	#eeeeee
Neutral text color	#666666
Neutral background color	#dddddd
Border color	#cccccc
Highlight color (for search results mainly)	#ffff99
Color for the very background (behind the content box)	#fbfaf9
The general link color	#2b73b7
The color for links to existing pages	#008800
The color for links to non-existing pages	#dd3300
The width of the full site (can be any length unit: %, px, em, ...)	75em
The width of the sidebar, if any (can be any length unit: %, px, em, ...)	16em
Below screensizes of this width, the site switches to tablet mode	800px
Below screensizes of this width, the site switches to phone mode	480px

Preview changes   Reset current changes

Save changes

Figure 12. *The Template Style Settings page allows you to change the absolute and relative widths of the wiki page and the sidebar.*

The third and fourth last settings define the width of the full site and the percentage of the sidebar width. You can use any type of HTML page measurement; if you're not familiar, percentages are generally easiest.

The defaults are 75 and 16 em, which turn out to be 100% and 21%. As you can see in **Figure 13**, the sidebar has a lot of unnecessary room.

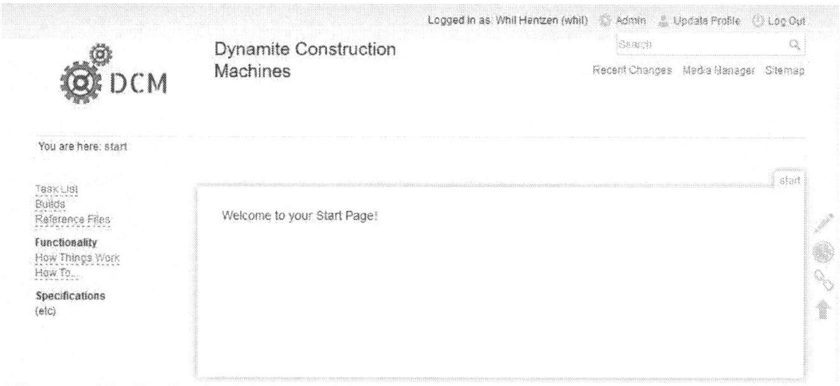

Figure 13. Default sidebar width.

First off, let's switch the units to percentages, so we see 100 and 21. Then we can fool around to see what more appropriate percentages are. Changing to 100 and 12 provides just enough room on the sidebar and way more room for content, as shown in **Figure 14**.

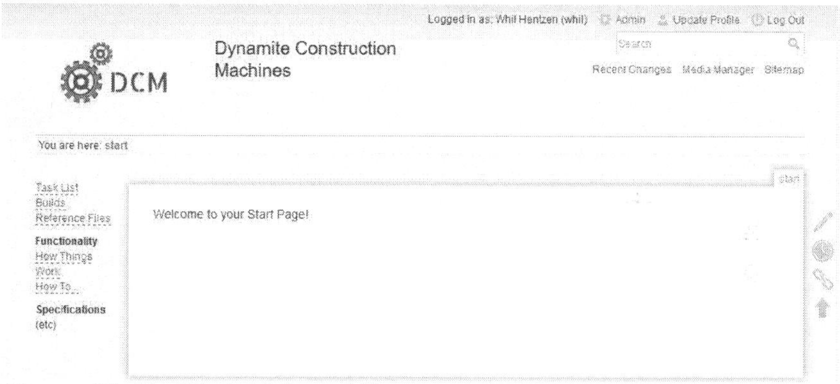

Figure 14. Modified sidebar width.

As you add more items to the sidebar, you may find that you need to change the widths, and you can simply go back to the Template Style Settings page and make adjustments.

You'll notice that the sidebar link is missing from the Start page in Figure 13. I removed it both to clean up the screenshot, and to show that you probably don't want the sidebar link generally editable.

That doesn't mean you won't need to edit it yourself. Look at the URL in your browser address bar, and notice it contains the string

```
doku.php?id=
```

When you navigate from one page to another, the name of the file becomes the "**id**" parameter. Using 'sidebar', like so:

```
doku.php?id=sidebar
```

will open the sidebar page.

7. The Installer in Detail

The choices provided in the installer can be confusing at first. After you've done a few installs, you get the hang of things, but when you're starting out, it's good to have a place where each choice, and the ramifications of those choices, is spelled out explicitly. Here's the place.

In chapters 3 and 4, we blew through the selections in the Installer fairly quickly. You probably are wondering "What about those other choices in the Installer?" and don't want to thumb all the way through to Chapter 33 to find out. Now it's time to discuss the other choices in the Installer and what the ramifications of those choices are.

Access Control Lists (ACL) Concepts

While one of the fundamental intents of a wiki is community editing of the pages, this doesn't necessarily mean that just any ol' traveler who wanders by can be considered part of the community. Particularly for DokuWiki, which was built for software documentation, it's important to be able to restrict who the community consists of, and what rights those members have.

As a result, DokuWiki uses a mechanism called Access Control Lists to allow the administrator to restrict access to the wiki as needed. This restriction may be as light as simply requiring a visitor to register before gaining access, or as sophisticated as organizing users into groups and assigning different rights (read-only, edit pages, create pages, etc.) to different areas of the wiki to each group.

The implementation of ACLs in DokuWiki is a two-step process. First, you choose whether to use ACLs or not. If you choose not, the game is over - you've got a wide open wiki with absolutely no security or restrictions - not even an administrator. If you do enable ACLs, you then have a second step to take - choosing how to structure the wiki - from wide open to completely closed or somewhere in between. I'll cover each of these permutations in the rest of this chapter.

Storage of installation and configuration settings

Installation and configuration settings are stored in a set of files in the /conf folder. I'll cover these settings in detail in Chapter 8, but here's the nickel tour so you can see how the various ACL options are stored as settings.

The 'acl.auth.php' file contains the Access Control Lists themselves. Except for the most extreme circumstances, you'll not edit this file yourself; instead, you'll use a tool called the ACL Manager (**plugin:acl**) to do so.

The 'users.auth.php' file contains the user set up to access the wiki. For example, once you create an administrator or a regular user, this information is stored in users.auth.php. Again, except for the most extreme circumstances, you'll not edit this file directly; instead, you'll use the User Manager (**plugin:usermanager**).

Hentzenwerke Publishing, Inc.
books@hentzenwerke.com • www.hentzenwerke.com

If you're editing these files in Windows, you should note that the default encoding for these files have Unix file endings, and won't look right in Microsoft Notepad. Use an editor that can respect a variety of line ending settings. My personal preference is Notepad++.

Finally, the 'local.php' file contains configuration settings. You've already run across three of these - the default language, the name of the wiki and whether or not ACL is enabled. The configuration settings are covered in greater detail in Chapter 8.

Option 1: Enable ACL checkbox deselected

Our first option is to deselect the Enable ACL checkbox. If you do so, you've created a wide-open wiki with no users, no restrictions, no nothing. Totally open to anyone who wanders by. All the rest of the controls on the Install page disappear, as shown in **Figure 1**.

Figure 1. *Enable ACL unchecked*

After you click 'Save' and continue on, you'll bypass the Login page and arrive at the Welcome screen, as shown in Chapter 5, Figure 1.

Notice that there is no "Login" button on this page as there was in Figure 6 of Chapter 3. Additionally, there is no way to enter the administration interface, which means that all configuration must be done manually by editing the DokuWiki configuration files in a text editor. If you don't need any access restrictions, you should still enable ACL and choose the "Open Wiki" option in the installer, which is covered in the next section.

Easy to use, not-so-easy to administer. But since we're working on private software documentation, this choice is not for us. The next three choices all feature the "Enable ACL" checkbox selected and one of the three options in the "Initial ACL policy" combo selected.

Under the hood: If you look in the 'conf' folder after deselecting ACL, you won't see acl.auth.php or users.auth.php files, and in local.php, there will be two settings - one for the default language and a second for the name of the wiki.

```
$conf['title'] = 'Dynamite Construction Machines';
$conf['lang'] = 'en';
```

There won't be a setting having to do with ACL. The absence of the setting means DokuWiki won't do any checking to ACL.

Option 2: Enable ACL, policy: open wiki

This option creates a wiki that is completely open, but an administrator account created and has user accounts enabled but not required. Usually, the only user account created is a super user who performs administrative tasks like configuration. See **Figure 2**.

Figure 2. *ACL enabled but wiki completely open.*

We've already seen what this permutation looks like. Figure 3 in Chapter 3 shows the Installer page with Enable ACL checked (yes, it's basically the same as Figure 2 here) and once done with the Installer page, you'll see the Login page and the Welcome page (Figures 6 and 7 in Chapter 3.)

Once at the Welcome page, we can sneak a peak under the hood. The local.php configuration file now contains two new entries.

```
$conf['useacl'] = 1;
$conf['superuser'] = '@admin';
```

The first option indicates that ACL is enabled, while the second assigns superuser capabilities to anyone who is a member of the 'admin' group.

Additionally, the acl.auth.php and users.auth.php files are created. (Finally!) The contents of the acl.auth.php file looks like this:

```
*              @ALL          8
```

This string means that all members of the group "ALL" (which is everyone) can read, create and edit pages, and that there will be a login button to allow a superuser to perform administrative tasks. The contents of this file will change in the next two configurations.

The users.auth.php file contains a single line like this:

```
whil:062e8c8d742d927sf7:Whil Hentzen:whil@whilhentzen.com:admin,user
```

This file contains the credentials of all users who have accounts; right now, only one user has an account - the super user who did the original install.

At this point, the wiki is completely open for editing by anyone who happens by. The only reason one would need to log in is to perform administrative tasks. Administration includes tasks like setting configuration options, managing templates, installing plugins, and adding additional users.

User accounts, even in an open wiki, are useful for attribution - so people can see who contributes useful material to the wiki - and so that users can receive notifications of when pages are changed (called page subscriptions.)

Option 3: Enable ACL, public wiki

The third choice in the Initial ACL policy combo is "public wiki", which, as it explains, allows anyone to read the contents of the wiki, but allows only logged in users to make changes. See **Figure 3**.

Figure 3. *Setting the Initial ACL policy to 'Public wiki' in the DokuWiki Installer.*

When you've set a wiki's Initial ACL policy to Public Wiki, and you open a wiki page, you'll see it won't look a lot different than an Open wiki page. The one change you might notice is the top button on the toolbar on the far right. With an open wiki, you've got an edit icon; here, you've got a view icon, because you've got to log in before being allowed to edit pages. Additionally, there are some changes under the hood.

The contents of the acl.auth.php file have changed in this configuration.

```
*            @ALL          1
*            @user         8
```

These settings say that all can read (setting = 1), but you must log in to create/edit pages (setting = 8).

The contents of the other two /conf files haven't changed. 'local.php' still contains the same contents as for an Open wiki and the 'users.auth.php' file is also the same as for an Open wiki - a single entry for the original super user defined in the Installer screen.

Option 4: Enable ACL, closed wiki

Here's where it gets interesting. Selecting the last choice in the Initial ACL policy combo box will result in a new look once you finish with the Installer. When you first navigate to the site, you'll get the Login page, and then once you log in, the Welcome page as we've seen in previous chapters.

All visitors must click "Login" and then enter their username and password credentials to gain access to the wiki - even if all they want to do is read pages.

Underneath the hood, the contents of the acl.auth.php file have changed.

```
*               @ALL        0
*               @user       8
```

These strings mean that all must log in before reading, editing or creating content (setting = 0).

The local.php and users.auth.php files remain the same.

From our brief exposure to ACL files, it appears that each line contains two components. The first is the name of the group and the second is a number that controls the permissions of the members of that group. In reality, things are somewhat more complex – see **acl** on dokuwiki.org.

Comparison of options

What if you chose one configuration and then realized you really wanted a different one? Since text files contain all of the configuration options, you can switch between ACL permutations by editing the acl.auth.php file. Here's a table that describes the basic differences.

Type	acl.auth.php Contents		Meaning
Open	`*`	`@ALL` 8	All can read and edit
Public	`*` `*`	`@ALL` 1 `@user` 8	All can read Must log in to edit
Closed	`*` `*`	`@ALL` 0 `@user` 8	Must log in to read or edit

After you've made the desired changes, you'll likely need to refresh the page. If you've really munged things up, you can just delete the local.php, users.auth.php and acl.auth.php files and go back to the DokuWiki installer:

```
http://localhost/<path_to_DokuWiki_root>/install.php
```

(You may have deleted install.php as suggested after you completed installation. In this case, you can re-upload it from your local copy.) Note that if you try to cheat and just hit your back button until you get to the Installer page, make a change, and then continue forward again as if no one was looking - without deleting the files - you'll get an error courtesy of a page that looks like **Figure 4.**

Figure 4. *Rerunning the DokuWiki installer without deleting the core config files generates an error page.*

Greeted with the page in Figure 4, you can hit your Back button to get to the Installer page again, *now* delete the files, and then continue on.

Saving your settings

By the way, if you've already done a bunch of configuring or added a bunch of users, your local.php file will be chock full of custom settings, and there'll be a lot of data in your users.auth.php file. Should you try to rerun the Installer, it will detect the configuration file with settings in it and complain. One solution is to rename those files temporarily and let the Installer create new empty ones for you, then set those empty files aside and name your own copies back to their original names. A better solution would be to put the conf\ folders under source code control so you can try out different options and use commit/rollback to move between them. Technically speaking, you shouldn't ever have to rerun the Installer.

Hentzenwerke Publishing, Inc.
books@hentzenwerke.com • www.hentzenwerke.com

Cleaning up

Once you're done with installation to your satisfaction, it's good practice to delete the install.php file. You've got the original in your dw_masters folder, right?

Conclusion

Restricting access to your wiki is a critical step in setting it up. Our sample wiki contains, at the least, valuable information that isn't appropriate to be released into the wild, and, very possibly, trade secrets and other confidential information. Thus, controlling who gets access is a process that you need to address early on, and become proficient at it. Using and configuring ACLs provide this capability.

8. Important Configuration Options

Like the characters in Animal Farm, all configuration settings are important, but some are more important than others. And the more important ones have achieved that status because, as a software developer, you're likely going to want to tweak them for your wiki. In this chapter, I'll discuss a dozen or two of the settings that you should be aware of sooner rather than later, and then show you what's going on with configuration settings under the hood.

In preceding chapters, I've mentioned configuration settings here and there, and then directed you to this chapter, where all would be revealed. Being a curious sort of reader, you may have already peeked ahead and opened up the Configuration Manager - and promptly freaked out, seeing a zillion settings. Way too many to absorb in one sitting. As a software developer using DokuWiki, which ones might you be most interested in? Don't know. But I can tell you which ones I've found immediately useful.

Accessing the Configuration Manager

Configuration is done as a superuser (any of them). Log in as a superuser (at this point, the name of the superuser you entered on the Installer page in Figure 3 in Chapter 2), and you'll see an 'Admin' link in the top right of any page. Click that link and you'll get a page with various administrative menu options, as shown in **Figure 1**.

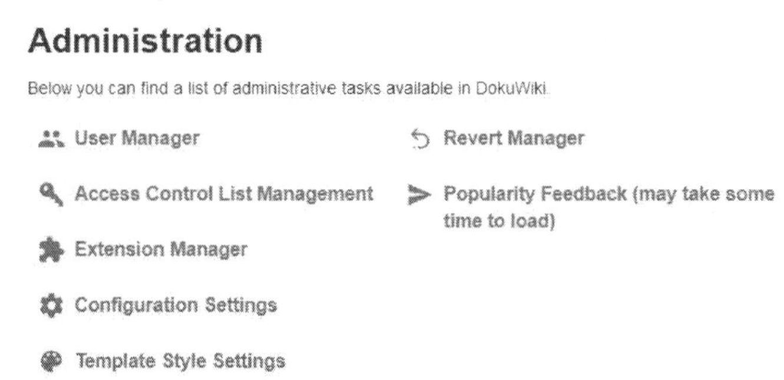

Administration

Below you can find a list of administrative tasks available in DokuWiki.

∴ User Manager	↺ Revert Manager
⚲ Access Control List Management	➤ Popularity Feedback (may take some time to load)
⚙ Extension Manager	
⚙ Configuration Settings	
⊕ Template Style Settings	

Figure 1. *The Administration menu.*

The option second from the bottom, "Configuration Settings", opens up the Configuration Manager. But let's take a quick tour of the Admin options first.

"User Manager" as you can imagine is where you maintain users – add, edit and delete them. Details are covered on the **plugin:usermanager** topic on dokuwiki.org.

"Access Control List Management" allows you to select which types of actions (read/edit/create/upload/delete) the users (either individually or as members of a group) are allowed to execute. This option was mentioned in Chapter 7.

Plugins are separate pieces of code, ranging from simple scripts to full blown applications, fitted into DokuWiki that extend the DokuWiki functionality. "Extension Manager" (formerly "Manage Plugins") allows you to download and install these applications as well as activate/deactivate and uninstall them. Again, a complex topic that gets its own chapter. See Chapter 12.

Templates are masks that control how your wiki looks and behaves. They're managed in one of the tabs on the Extension Manager page, but the settings for the current template are maintained via "Template Style Settings".

One of the downsides of having an editable Web site open to the world is that spammers may happen across it and attempt to fill the pages full of their nonsense and filth. Fortunately, it's relatively easy to identify a single page that has been modified; on the flip side, not so easy to go through a wiki of hundreds or thousands of pages and get rid of the spam content on each of them. The "Revert Manager" allows you to search your entire wiki for pages that contain a specific term and then revert pages found back to a previously known good state.

Finally, the "Popularity Feedback" link allows you to send configuration information about your wiki installation to the DokuWiki developers in order to provide better information about how DokuWiki is being used in order to aid future development. If you're concerned about privacy or secrecy due to the content of your wiki, no worries. It'll show you all the data that is collected - all of it is anonymous - no IP addresses, serial numbers, or shoe sizes. And, again, it's completely up to you - but all you need to do is push the 'Send' button on the page to make it happen. Imagine if you had detailed metrics about how your users used your applications - wouldn't that help your future work? Go ahead, give it a shot!

You'll notice I skipped over the Configuration Settings link; it runs a plugin called the Configuration Manager, and opens the Configuration Manager page, the top of which is shown in **Figure 2**.

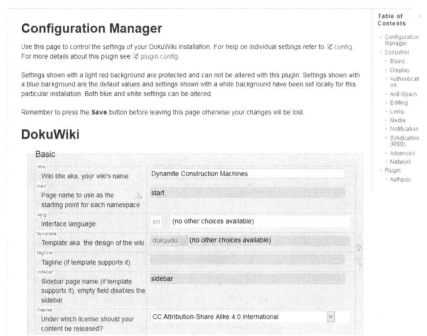

Figure 2. *The DokuWiki Configuration Manager.*

I kept it for last because it's what we're going to be talking about for the rest of this chapter. There are lots of goodies here. Let's explore for a moment.

Page contents

First of all, you may see up to three different background colors of settings on the page. They each mean something different:

Red: protected setting, can't be changed through the plugin. (See the subsection "Protecting settings" later in this section for details.)

Blue: Default value, can be changed.

White: User-modified value, from the blue default.

As the top of the page says, individual settings are described at www.dokuwiki.com/config and details about the plugin that drives this page are described at www.dokuwiki.com/plugin:config. I suggest you scan through the config page to get an idea of the various options; no need to simply repeat all that here.

Additionally, in this chapter, I'll discuss the values of settings from the point of view of the Configuration Manager - such as "Checked to auto-generate passwords, unchecked to let users choose their own passwords". The config page delineates the values of the settings from the point of view of the data physically stored in the local.php file - such as "1 to auto-generate passwords, 0 to allow users choose their own passwords".

You'll also note that some settings are flagged with a yellow triangle; others with a red circle, and yet others with a padlock, as shown in **Figure 3**.

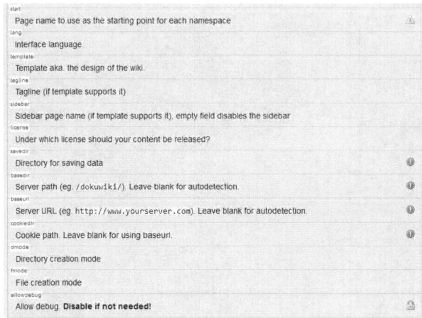

Figure 3. *Various flags to indicate cautions about settings.*

The yellow triangle warns you that changing the value for this option could cause unexpected or unintended behavior, while the red circle is a sterner warning that changing the value could wreck your wiki altogether. For example, changing the name of your starting namespace from the default 'start' to another value could make the contents of an existing start page disappear (I'll discuss how to deal with that situation shortly) while changing the directory for saving data could prevent users from accessing the wiki altogether.

The padlock flags settings that can possibly pose a security risk if set incorrectly.

Organization of Configuration Settings

There are eleven groups of settings in an 'out of the box' installation.

- Basic
- Display
- Authentication
- Anti-Spam
- Editing
- Links

- Media
- Notification
- Syndication (RSS)
- Advanced
- Network

(Installing additional modules - plugins or templates - sometimes adds additional groups of settings.) These groups are organized functionally; as a result, there are a couple of groups we'll spend a lot of time in, and others that we'll ignore completely. Within the groups, I'll discuss the options I feel are most important.

Notice that the Table of Contents box in the upper right corner of the page lists the names of these eleven (or more) groups. The Table of Contents will dynamically change when new groups of settings are added to the configuration files.

A quick peek under the hood

As you might recall, the choices you made in the Installer result in the creation of and content of files in the 'conf' folder. Changes you make in the Configuration Manager modify those files as well. Two of the files deal with configuration.

dokuwiki.php

The dokuwiki.php file is the master configuration file for DokuWiki. Opening it up and scanning through it (don't make any changes!) is rather informational; each setting is described and many have suggested defaults.

local.php

OK, if you're not supposed to make changes to the dokuwiki.php file, where *do* you make them? The local.php file provides a vehicle for you to override settings in dokuwiki.php instead of changing the master. DokuWiki reads both files; if it sees a setting in local.php, DokuWiki overrides the matching (default) setting in dokuwiki.php.

This mechanism is structured this way so that you can specify your own configuration settings that won't be overridden or broken when the next update to DokuWiki comes along and replaces the dokuwiki.php file.

When you use the Configuration Manager to specify your own settings, they are written to the local.php file.

Setting names

Each setting on the Configuration Manager page has two names on the left side of the setting box. For example, the setting for the name of the wiki is "Wiki Title, aka you wiki's name". Up and to the left of the "Wiki Title" text, in a smaller font, is a second text string, in this case, 'title'. This string is the setting name that you'll see in the dokuwiki.php and local.php files. (In earlier versions of DokuWiki, the setting name wasn't displayed - this addition is truly welcome!)

Hentzenwerke Publishing, Inc.
books@hentzenwerke.com • www.hentzenwerke.com

Saving (and Resetting)

You have to click the 'Save' button on the bottom of the page in order to commit your changes to the local.php file. Upon save, the local.php file gets a new timestamp which invalidates all caches immediately. However, you may find that the changes you make aren't necessarily visible immediately. It is usually the browser cache that contains old copies of pages. At worst, exiting DokuWiki and starting it up again will take care of this.

The 'Reset' button acts as an 'Undo' to any changes you've made since last clicking the Save button. For example, suppose you changed the Start page name to 'home sweet home', and then clicked Save. Then you discovered that some of the users of the wiki didn't appreciate this whimsical touch, so you changed it to 'home'. But before you saved the change to 'home', the humourless malcontent who didn't like 'home sweet home' was taken off this project, so you decided to keep 'home sweet home'. Click 'Reset' and the Start page name is now back to 'home sweet home'.

Protecting settings

Earlier I mentioned that settings displayed with a red background can't be modified. You may be wondering which settings those would be - and if you scrolled through the entire Configuration Manager page, you saw that there weren't any. These types of settings - protected - have to be set up manually.

In order to protect a setting from ever being changed, create a text file named local.protected.php that looks just like local.php. This file goes in the 'conf' folder alongside the other DokuWiki configuration files. In it, include only the settings you want to prevent from being changed. Suppose you wanted to protect the Wiki title from ever being changed. The following file would do so:

```
<?php
/*
 * Dokuwiki's Main Configuration File - Protected Local Settings
 */
$conf['title'] = 'Dynamite Construction Machines';
```

Then, when anyone opened the Configuration Manager, the Wiki title setting would have a light red background, and couldn't be changed. See **Figure 4**.

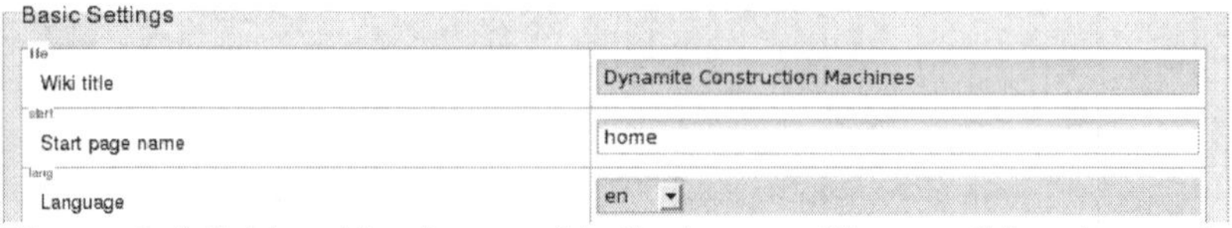

Figure 4. A light red background indicates a setting can't be changed.

Hentzenwerke Publishing, Inc.
books@hentzenwerke.com • www.hentzenwerke.com

Basic Settings

The Basic Settings apply to the entire wiki. I've mentioned the Wiki title; here's where it's located. Others of interest include Start page name, Template, and Directory for saving data.

Wiki title

As you saw, the title of the wiki is set during installation, and I admonished you to pick a good title. What if you choose badly? Or, more likely, you choose wisely but your boss or customer now has a 'better' idea. You can change the title that shows up in the upper right corner of each page with the wiki title setting under Basic Settings.

Start page name

The first thing I do in the Configuration Manager (I set the Wiki title during installation) is change the "Start page name" from 'start' to 'home'. You know, like a 'home page'. Just my own personal preference.

Remember that the 'start.txt' page on disk isn't created until you enter content into it and save. However, if you've entered content into 'start.txt', saved it, and then changed the "Start page name" setting to 'home', 'start.txt' will be orphaned. So I suggest you change this setting immediately if you intend on doing so. If you're already too far gone, and you have access to the file system where your DokuWiki files are stored, you can manually rename 'start.txt' to 'home.txt'.

Template

One of DokuWiki's great strengths is that its look and feel can be altered and extended through the use of additional PHP scripts called templates. You are probably familiar with the concept of templates that alter the appearance of an application - DokuWiki's templates take that one step further; some templates actually provide additional functionality as well as a new pretty face.

A template is added to DokuWiki simply by downloading and unzipping it into its own folder under the 'lib/tpl' folder. DokuWiki then parses the list of folders under 'lib/tpl' and populates the Template setting combo box with that list. By default, DokuWiki comes only with the 'default' template displayed in the combo box (which is why it's disabled), and a prompt stating that 'no other choices are available'.

To switch from one template to another (supposing that there is more than one available), just choose the desired template in the combo box.

Templates are covered in more detail in Chapter 11, Your First Template.

Directory for saving data

DokuWiki data is stored in a folder named 'data', located in the DokuWiki root, which contains a half dozen or so subfolders, including 'attic', 'cache', 'media', 'meta' and 'pages'. These folders, being located under the DokuWiki root, look like they're Web-accessible due to their location, but in fact, are protected by an .htaccess file that denies access. Depending on your environment, you still may prefer to have your data located elsewhere - at the very least, outside of the public Web folder, at the extreme, on a different physical server.

This setting points DokuWiki to its data, and thus, you can change the setting should you decide to relocate your data. The default value is './data'. Here's how to change it.

Dedicated server

A typical Apache Web root folder layout for a dedicated server machine running Apache might look like this (in part):

```
/var/www/html
/var/www/html/dw_installation_one
/var/www/html/dw_installation_one\data
/var/www/html/dw_installation_two
/var/www/html/dw_installation_two\data
```

Everything under the 'html/' folder is Web accessible, including the data folders under each installation. In order to keep your data out of the reach, you could create a folder specifically for data under the 'www' folder, like so:

```
/var/www/data
```

and then add folders for each DokuWiki installation:

```
/var/www/data/installation_1
/var/www/data/installation_2
```

Then, in the 'Directory for saving data' setting for DokuWiki installation #1, you'd enter

```
../../data/installation_1
```

and then move everything under '/var/www/html/dw_installation_one/data' to '/var/www/data/installation_1'. In essence, the 'data' folder under 'installation_one' becomes the 'data\installation_1' folder. Same thing for other DokuWiki installations. If your Linux is running SELinux or similar security features, you may need to invoke additional magic to get the Apache process (in which PHP runs) to read/write the data directories.

Shared host

If you're running DokuWiki on a shared host, the concepts are the same; the syntax is a bit different. For example, many ISPs provide a folder under /var/www/html for each customer running on that box. For example:

```
/var/www/html/customer_one
/var/www/html/customer_two
/var/www/html/customer_three
```

That folder ('/var/www/html/customer_one') becomes the root folder for the customer, with a number of default folders already created for you ('customer_one'), like so:

```
/var/www/html/customer_one/config
/var/www/html/customer_one/public_ftp
/var/www/html/customer_one/public_html
/var/www/html/customer_one/scripts
```

When you would log in, you'd see

```
/
/config
/public_ftp
/public_html
/scripts
```

and so on.

The 'public_html' folder would be mapped to Apache as Web accessible - in fact, it would be the Web root folder - while the rest would not be. Your DokuWiki installations would reside under the 'public_html', like so:

```
/public_html/dw_install_one
/public_html/dw_install_two
```

and so on. You could create a 'data' folder under your root folder, on the same level as, say, '/config', thus placing it outside of the 'public_html' folder's reach:

```
/
/config
/data
/public_html
```

And, just like with a dedicated server, you would then create individual folders for each DokuWiki installation:

```
/data/installation_1
/data/installation_2
```

Inside DokuWiki, the 'Directory for saving data' setting would be

```
../../data/installation_1
```

just like for a dedicated server, since the new data folder is, relatively, in the same position.

Display Settings

The Display Settings configuration options provide a lot of customization capability; your preferences are likely to be different than mine. Still, the way the wiki appears to users affects how they interact with it, and thus what they do with it, so it still comes down to functionality.

Recent changes

The 'Number of entries per page in the recent changes' setting controls how many items are displayed on a single page when you click the "Recent changes' button on a wiki page. This setting also determines how many items are returned in XML syndication.

Number of breadcrumbs/Hierarchical breadcrumbs

The other settings I change immediately are these ones, also under "Display Settings". I set the "Number of 'trace' Breadcrumbs" to 0, then select the "Hierarchical breadcrumbs" checkbox. The first action removes the trace row, and the second action will display a second row of links under the "Trace" row at the top of each page. See **Figure 5** to see both rows.

Figure 5. *Hierarchical and Trace rows.*

While "Trace" is handy to see where you've been, "Hierarchical breadcrumbs" will display the page at each level that you've visited to get to where you are at. For software documentation, which is typically arranged in a traditional hierarchy, this can be very handy.

Suppose your main wiki page has the following topics:

```
Welcome...
General Description
Functional Specifications
Technical Specifications
Architecture
Project Plans
```

Under General Description, you have the following pages:

```
Executive Summary
Line of Business Description
Specific Industry Terminology
```

When a user navigates lands on the Executive Summary page, the "Hierarchical breadcrumbs" row will show

```
You are here: home > General Description > Executive Summary
```

no matter how they got there.

The 'Trace' row of breadcrumbs, on the other hand, shows the last pages visited, like so:

```
architecture » data » technical_specifications » home »
general_description » executive_summary
```

Some folks might want to remove the 'Trace' row of breadcrumbs but are initially stymied by the lack of a checkbox to turn it on or off like the Hierarchical breadcrumbs setting. This is accomplished by setting the "Number of breadcrumbs" to 0.

While completely separate in terms of how they work, these settings can be used in tandem by the user in order to most efficiently navigate through a web of pages, so you might want to leave them both on.

Reveal full path of pages in the footer

The name of the file on disk behind the page displayed in the browser is displayed in the lower right corner of each wiki page. **Figure 6** shows that

```
start.txt
```

is the name of the current file.

start.txt · Last modified: 2017/08/28 08:26 by whil

Figure 6. The default footer just shows the path within the 'pages' folder.

Checking the "Reveal full path of pages in the footer" setting will cause the fully qualified path of the page to be displayed instead, as shown in **Figure 7**.

F:/Dropbox/Sites/DWS/dokuwiki/data/pages/start.txt · Last modified: 2017/08/28 08:26 by whil

Figure 7. *Setting 'Reveal full path of pages in the footer' displays the path back to the root of the drive.*

Note that this isn't just the path to the Web root - it's the fully qualified path on the box. So even if you're on a shared host, you'll see the path all the way back to the top level folder. While potentially useful for the administrator, and possibly helpful in a corporate environment where this feature gives people a feeling for where their DokuWiki data is physically stored, it's also a security risk in that it provides detailed knowledge about how the server is set up. Check this setting only if you are sure you know what you're doing.

Date format

Dates displayed on DokuWiki pages (such as in the footer, and with signatures) are formatted using PHP strftimefunction format. The default format string is

```
%Y/%m/%d %H:%M
```

which causes dates to be displayed like so:

```
2008/04/28 16:29
```

You can change the format using other PHP strftime function format meta-characters. For example, '%Y' represents the four digit year while '%y' will display just the last two digits. '%b' displays the three character abbreviation of the month ('Jan', 'Feb', etc.) while 'm' displays the two digit number of the month (including leading zeros) and '%d' displays the two digit number of the month (including leading zeros).

You can also provide your own separators between the various date and time components. The following string

```
%Y-%m-%d (%H:%M)
```

separates the date components with hyphens instead of slashes and puts the time in parenthesis. If you enter an incorrect string (say, forgetting the "%" before a character), your string will be just shown as is.

See http://us2.php.net/strftime for a complete list of format characters. (Type 'php strftime' in your browser address bar to get there quickly.)

Signature

As you saw in Chapter 4, the user can insert their 'signature' via the 'Signature' button in the editing toolbar. The format of the signature is determined via this setting. The '@MAIL@', '@NAME@' and '@DATE@' strings automatically insert those variables into the signature. You can also use the '@USER@' variable to display the user's login name instead of their full name. Much like the Date format setting, you can provide your own separators and other characters. Here's the full list of variables you can use:

Variable	Meaning
@DATE@	Current date/time formatted per the 'Date format' setting
@MAIL@	User's email address ("al@example.com")
@NAME@	User's full name ("Al Anxious")
@USER@	User's login name ("al")

You can also use strftime placeholders if you don't want to use the full @DATE@ format.

What to display when showing the user that last edited a page

If your wiki is set up so that all users must log in before editing a page, the page they edit will display their identity afterwards. Those of you familiar with Superhero lore are well aware, however, that their identify may simply be a cover, and not give another visitor enough information in order to contact them.

This option allows you, the administrator, to choose how that identity is displayed - either their login name, their full name (plain text or interwiki link), or their email address (either obfuscated or as a mailto link.) See **Figure 8**.

Figure 8. User identify display options.

Most options are immediately obvious, but the third, interwiki user link, may not be. It displays the user's full name as a link to that user's page on the wiki, as shown in **Figure 9**.

Last modified: 2017/08/28 08:26 by   Whil Hentzen

Figure 9. The user identity configured as an interwiki link.

If there isn't a user page yet, the link will be underlined just like any other page that's not been created.

Top level for table of contents/Maximum level/Maximum section edit level

These three are all related; if you want to change one, you may well want to change others.

The table of contents is the set of links in the upper right corner of each page. The links provide a visual map for the page as well as providing the ability to navigate (scroll) to a particular section in the page quickly. In Figure 2, the display of the configuration options, you'll see a link for each section of settings – this is the table of contents. The Table of Contents pulls its links from the various levels of section and subsection headings on the page.

The 'Top level for table of contents' setting determines the top level of heading that will be included in the table of contents. Normally, you'll want it set at '1', the default, but you may want it lower if you're using the biggest headings for other purposes.

The second determines how many levels of headings you want displayed in the table of contents. You'll likely want to change this if you've changed the Top level. You can also change the Maximum level to '0' if you don't want a table of contents displayed.

Finally, the 'Maximum section edit level' setting controls the display of the 'Edit' buttons that display throughout a page that has multiple headings. Again, if you've changed the 'Top level for table of contents' setting due to special page layout requirements, you may want to change this too. And like the 'Maximum level for table of contents' setting, a value of '0' for this will turn the 'Edit' buttons off.

Use CamelCase for links

DokuWiki uses a string enclosed in double brackets to designate a link to another page. Some other wikis use text strings that contain no spaces but a capital letter at the beginning of each word (called 'CamelCase') to designate a link. If you'd like to use CamelCase instead, select this setting. Note that doing so, and then changing back to the DokuWiki standard of double brackets may create orphan pages.

Authentication Settings

These settings all have to do with controlling access, restricting users, and generally handling security issues for your wiki.

Use access control lists

Remember back in the olden days, around the time you were installing DokuWiki? And the third setting you had to configure was whether or not to use ACL? Here's the checkbox for this setting. Details back in Chapter 7.

Autogenerate passwords

If you allow users to register themselves on the wiki (see "Disable DokuWiki actions" setting in the next section), you can choose whether or not to let them choose their own passwords. Checking this option will cause the system to automatically generate a password that is emailed to the user. The email looks something like this:

```
Hi Dave Dashing!

Here is your userdata for Dynamite Construction Machines at
http://www.example.com/dcm/

Login    : dave
Password : 728dfe7s21w

--
This mail was generated by DokuWiki at
http://www.example.com/dcm/
```

By the way, the email address this message COMES from is configured by the "Sender email address to use for automatic mails" setting in the Notification section.

Unchecking this option will cause a pair of text boxes to be displayed during registration; the first for the password and the second for the password confirmation. Email is not sent to the user in this scenario.

Authentication backend

Credentials, such as usernames and passwords, are, by default, stored in the users.auth.php file, in a format like so:

```
al:062e9c437b71c813b81fa907r39c766e:Al
Anxious:al@example.com:admin,user
```

A fairly common scenario occurs when user credentials already exist elsewhere, and you want to simply piggyback on that data instead of entering (and maintaining) it another time. This setting allows you to do so.

Password encryption method

By default, passwords are stored using smd5 encryption. You can choose a different method using this setting.

Default group

This setting is used in two scenarios. First, when a superuser adds a user to the wiki, they can manually specify which groups that user belongs to. If they don't specify any groups, the group named in this setting is used. Second, if users are allowed to register themselves, they will automatically be added to the group named in this setting.

Note that if this setting is blank, a user can be added but they won't be able to do anything once they log in. (I suspect you have a couple of users for who this scenario would be useful.)

Superuser/Manager

During installation, if you enabled ACLs, you added a user who was automatically defined as a superuser (administrator.) You can define other users as well as entire groups to also be superusers through this setting.

Users and/or groups specified in Manager options are given additional, but limited, capabilities in the Admin menu: Revert Manager and Popularity Feedback.

Both settings use the same syntax - usernames are entered 'as is' while groupnames are identified with an '@' before the name. Multiple entries are separated by commas. For example:

```
al, bob, @salesreps, @legal, zoe
```

In this example, 'al', 'bob' and 'zoe' are all usernames while 'salesreps' and 'legal' are names of groups. Note that the name entered in the default group setting is *not* preceded by an '@' sign.

Confirm profile changes with password

The "Update Profile" link in the upper right of the wiki allows the user to change their Full Name, Email address and password. If the "Confirm profile changes with password" setting is checked, an additional text box, "Confirm current password" is displayed in the User Profile page, and the user must enter their current password in order to change any of their data, as shown in **Figure 10**.

Update your account profile

You only need to complete those fields you wish to change. You may not change your user name.

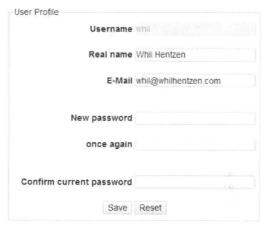

Figure 10. The Update Profile page when the "Confirm profile changes with password" setting is checked.

Allow permanent login cookies (remember me)

Some folks detest having to log in every time they visit the wiki, particularly if they're using it a lot, and even more so if it's an internal wiki accessed from their own private workstation. This option, checked by default, displays the "Remember me" checkbox on the Login page so that users can choose whether or not to have their login credentials remembered by their browser.

Disable DokuWiki Actions

By default, users have the ability to do all sorts of interesting things. Depending on your needs, you may not want to give them quite as much freedom. Checking an option in this section prevents all users from performing the action. See **Figure 11**.

☐ Backlinks		☐ Sitemap	
☐ Recent Changes		☐ Old revisions	
☐ Search		☐ Subscribe/Unsubscribe	
☑ Register		☐ Set new password	
☐ Update Profile		☐ Delete Own Account	
☐ Edit this page		☐ View source/Export Raw	
☐ Check		☐ XML Syndication (RSS)	

Other actions (comma separated)

Figure 11. *The Configuration Manager allows you to restrict users from performing certain actions.*

When you disable an action, the control that provides that action is simply removed from the interface. For example, checking the "Register" and "Old revisions" checkboxes cause those buttons to disappear from pages. Similarly, checking the "Update Profile" checkbox removes that link from the top of the wiki page.

The Register setting is checked by default, if the ACL setting is set to require logins.

Unchecking the Register and Set new password settings results in those options on the Login page, as shown in **Figure 12**.

Login

You are currently not logged in! Enter your authentication credentials below to log in. You need to have cookies enabled to log in.

Figure 12. *Register and Set new password options on the Login screen.*

Checking the "Register" and "Send new password" checkboxes remove them from the Login page, in a rather barren display, as shown in **Figure 13**.

Login

You are currently not logged in! Enter your authentication credentials below to log in. You need to have cookies enabled to log in.

Log in

Username	
Password	
	☐ Remember me
	Log In

***Figure 13**. Checking the "Send new password" and "Register" checkboxes in Disable DokuWiki actions remove both links from the Login page.*

This barren look is well-suited for wikis with tight security and/or a very limited group of users.

Unfortunately, you can't (easily) disable actions just for a certain group of users. It's all or nothing.

The "Other actions" textbox needs a bit of explanation. What the heck do you put in there? If you've been watching the URLs as you perform functions, you've noticed that they have the format

```
?do=SomeAction
```

For example, clicking the "Recent changes", "Index" and "Search" buttons (the last after entering "Herman Munster" in the search text box) produces the following URLs:

```
http://localhost/wh/dcm/doku.php/?do=recent
http://localhost/wh/dcm/doku.php/home?do=index
http://localhost/wh/dcm/doku.php/?do=search&id=Herman+Munster
```

Thus, any "do" action you would want to restrict is fair game for this text box. Checkboxes for common actions are already provided. For example, suppose you wanted to be ornery and prevent users from clicking on the "Show page" button (the top button on the right side toolbar.) Entering "show" for this setting would result in an error message to be displayed as shown in **Figure 14**.

***Figure 14**. The results of restricting an action.*

It's probably not productive to do a lot of guesswork as to the names of actions; instead, head on over to the **devel:action_modes** wiki topic for a rather complete list. I might note that using actions other than those already shown as checkbox-enabled in Figure 11 are probably useful only for developers during testing.

Anti-Spam Settings

The Anti-Spam settings are all useful and, to my way of thinking, their defaults are all set up properly. If I had my druthers, I might wish for a second obfuscation option for email addresses, as the one provided (hex encoding) is common enough that a fair number of bots takes it into account, but that's just a nit.

Editing Settings

This section contains a number of unrelated settings having to do with options that users will access while using their pages.

Automatically save a draft while editing

Checked by default, this setting controls whether or not drafts are saved, as described in Chapter 10.

Allow embedded HTML/PHP

These guys provide the ability for users to incorporate HTML and PHP code directly in pages. Obviously these can be a huge security risk, so these should be off unless the access to your wiki is restricted. There are ways to include and display code without setting this option on.

Maximum age for lock files/cache

Also described in Chapter 10, these settings allow you to control how long locks last (15 * 60 = 15 minutes, by default) and when cached pages are replaced (60 * 60 * 24 = one day).

Link Settings

These settings allow you to determine how links on wiki pages are handled. By default, a link on a page opens the new page in the same window. If you want a link to open a new window, enter '_blank' for that setting. See **Figure 15**.

Figure 15. Forcing internal links to open in new windows.

If a setting is '_self' or empty, the link will open in the same window.

Media Settings

In this context, media refers to all sorts of files - images, PDF files, audio files, and so on.

Maximum size

This setting configures how much data from external servers will be downloaded for caching and resizing external images. It is disabled by default, but you may want to set it to a limiting size like 500kb to 1mb for regular purposes, or much higher if you're using the wiki as a document repository.

Notification Settings

These settings control how the wiki administrator and users are notified about events that go with the wiki.

Allow users to subscribe to page changes by email

Once you're hip deep into using a wiki, the question "How do I know when someone else has made changes to a page that I'm interested in?" arises. The answer is page subscription. Logged in users can choose to 'subscribe' to pages, which means they'll be notified (via email) when the contents of the page have changed.

There are actually two pieces to this - a user can choose to be notified when a specific page is modified, or when any of the pages belonging to a namespace (think 'folder', remember?) have been modified, or when a page is added to or deleted from a namespace.

Checking this setting adds the envelope icon in the right hand toolbar. Clicking in opens the Subscription Management page as shown in **Figure 16.**

Hentzenwerke Publishing, Inc.
books@hentzenwerke.com • www.hentzenwerke.com

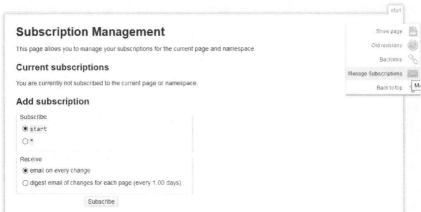

Figure 16. The 'Subscription Management' page allows the current user to subscribe to pages and namespaces, and lists current subscriptions.

Always send change notifications to this email address

If a user has subscribed to a page or a namespace (see the next section for details), they'll get an email each time the page is changed. This email looks like this:

```
A page in your DokuWiki was added or changed. Here are the details:

Date        : 2008-09-14 (15:05)
Browser     : Mozilla/5.0 (X11; U; Linux i686; en-US; rv:1.8.1.6)
Gecko/20070812 Remi/2.0.0.6-1.fc6.remi Firefox/2.0.0.6 pango-text
IP-Address  : 127.0.0.1
Hostname    : yo-yo-computer
Old Revision: http://localhost/wh/dcm/doku.php?id=home&rev=1220635224
New Revision: http://localhost/wh/dcm/doku.php?id=home
Edit Summary: Changed date, added new date
User        : tina

@@ -7,5 +7,6 @@
   [[Dates to remember]]

- <box>October 12, 2009 </box>
+ <box>October 17, 2009.</box>
+ <box>October 31, 2009.</box>
```

A copy of every change notification is sent to a central address as well, typically an administrator's email. This setting identifies this address.

Always send info on newly registered users to this email address

If Disable DokuWiki actions | Register is unchecked, users can register themselves. When they do, they'll get a confirmation email. Additionally, the address entered in this setting will get an email telling about the new member. The email looks like this by default:

```
A new user has registered. Here are the details:

User name   : donna
Full name   : Donna the Tester
E-mail      : donna@example.com

Date        : 2008-07-26 (18:20)
Browser     : Mozilla/5.0 (X11; U; Linux i686; en-US; rv:1.8.1.6)
Gecko/20070812 Remi/2.0.0.6-1.fc6.remi Firefox/2.0.0.6 pango-text
IP-Address  : 127.0.0.1
Hostname    : yo-yo-computer

--
This mail was generated by DokuWiki at
http://localhost/wh/dcm/
```

typically this address will be that of an administrator of the wiki.

Sender email address to use for automatic mails

DokuWiki sends out emails for a variety of functions, including user registration, password reminders, and page subscriptions ('change notifications'). Except for certain spam generators, an email has to have both a 'from' and a 'to'. This setting controls the "from" address for all DokuWiki-generated email. Since DokuWiki doesn't know your email address, the setting will initially be blank. If blank, DokuWiki will use the name and address of the Web server user. Typically, this is something like

```
www-data@localhost.localdomain
```

For example, before I configure this setting, page subscription notifications were sent from

```
whil@localhost.localdomain
```

and when those notifications were sent to a gmail account, they ended up in the Spam folder. Big surprise, huh?

Since DokuWiki will send the email out using this address, you'll want to make sure your mail server doesn't block this address!

Syndication (RSS) Settings

If you're an RSS user, these settings allow you to control how the wiki generates information.

Advanced Settings

Show the Configuration Manager to a dozen programmers and 110% of them will automatically gravitate toward the 'Advanced Settings' section first. I know I sure did.

Check for updates and security warnings?

If you have this setting checked, updates to DokuWiki will be innocuously announced on every page of DokuWiki installations when an administrator is logged in. See **Figure 17**.

Figure 17. *Updates to DokuWiki are announced via a notice on wiki pages.*

Nice URLs

Every time I see this expression, I think of reassuring an angry pit bull, saying, "Nice doggy! Nice doggy!" while slowly backing away. "Nice URLs" refers to the format of the DokuWiki URL in the address bar. By default, a DokuWiki URL looks like this:

```
http://localhost/wh/dcm/doku.php?id=home
```

Some folks don't like this appearance, particularly when additional parms get added on:

```
http://localhost/wh/dcm/doku.php?id=home&purge=true
```

The choices in the Nice URLs setting allow you to rewrite URLs via a modified .htaccess file or through DokuWiki's internal engine. The results look like this, respectively:

```
http://localhost/wh/dcm/home
http://localhost/wh/dcm/doku.php/home
```

There have been instances where, depending on the configuration of the Web server, messing up this setting can restrict access to the wiki completely. If this happens to you, never fear; just edit your DokuWiki config file by hand, removing the 'userewrite' setting, and all will be good.

See the **rewrite** topic on the wiki for additional tips and tricks.

Network Settings

The network settings can be organized into three groups: first, handling a proxy server for outbound connections, second, dealing with an ISP that has restrictive permissions for mkdir() and rmdir() functions (which causes problems when you want to add or remove namespaces), and third, configuring FTP.

I have not needed to modify the settings for any of these scenarios, but the wiki pages are chock full of information for these circumstances.

Plugin

DokuWiki comes configured out of the box with Auth PDO so that you can authenticate users against a SQL database. The settings in this section allow you to configure the connection and communication with the database.

Conclusion

As a software developer, you're in business because your customers want things their way, instead of the way things came out of the box. And so you're likely to want to configure software you use as well, and the multitude of configuration options available in DokuWiki allow you to do just that. But configuration is just the beginning. In the next two chapters, you're going to learn how to customize DokuWiki even further, with the use of Templates and Plugins.

9. User Editing and Page Formatting

While the ability to simply edit a Web page in a collaborative environment will thrill many a computer user for a while, eventually the excitement will wear off. No longer is just typing content in the edit box enough; users will want to make it look nice. This chapter covers dozens of ways to format the contents of DokuWiki pages.

When a dotted link is clicked, the user navigates to a place holder to a page that is yet to be created. For example, supposed the sidebar has a link for "Task List" as shown in **Figure 1**.

Figure 1. *A link to a yet-to-be-created page.*

Clicking on that link navigates to the placeholder page, as shown in **Figure 2**.

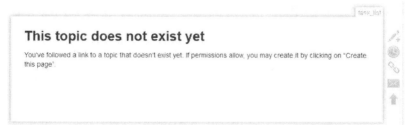

Figure 2. *Starting off with a page ready to be created.*

You can tell that this page placeholder is for the Task List link because the tab in the upper right corner has the name of the page.

As mentioned before, when a page hasn't been created yet, the top icon on the right consists of a pencil and a plus sign, indicating that the page needs to be added to the wiki. Clicking the icon creates an empty editing box as shown in **Figure 3**.

Figure 3. *An empty editing box.*

To start, let's look at some editing and formatting features. Note that the examples are shown in bold, monospaced font in order to set them off from the text; the actual results in a Web page will look different.

Creating paragraphs

Type text in the edit box. Type to the end of the box and your text will wrap to the next line automatically. The edit box will ignore single carriage returns, such that text like so:

```
This is one paragraph ended with a carriage return.
This is supposed to be a new paragraph but it won't be.
```

will end up looking like this:

```
This is one paragraph ended with a carriage return. This is supposed to
be a new paragraph but it won't be.
```

There are two ways to force a new paragraph. The first is to separate a paragraph and the succeeding paragraph with two carriage returns, like so:

```
This is one paragraph ended with a carriage return.
```

```
This is supposed to be a new paragraph and it will be.
```

to generate a result like this:

```
This is one paragraph ended with a carriage return.
This is supposed to be a new paragraph and it will be.
```

The other way is to end a line with special meta-characters - two backslashes –
to force a paragraph, like so:

```
This is one paragraph ended with a carriage return.\\
This is supposed to be a new line but not a new paragraph.
```

The result is the same:

```
This is one paragraph ended with a carriage return.
This is supposed to be a new line, but not a new paragraph.
```

However, the second method is discouraged. It's cumbersome to write and
semantically incorrect. Using true paragraphs encourages logical text structure,
differentiating between thoughts.

Changes

One of the secret strengths of DokuWiki is that it acts as a version control system
along with a collaborative document creation tool. As you edit a page, changes are
tracked by the system. Each time a user saves a page, the old version is archived via
a compressed file placed in the data/attic folder. Let's examine this mechanism in a
little more detail.

Documenting changes

As soon as you start typing in the edit box, you'll see that the "Edit summary" text
box under the edit box turns pink, as shown in **Figure 4**. This serves two purposes.
The first purpose is simply to alert you that you've made changes to the contents of
the edit box, much like 'edited' markers in other programs.

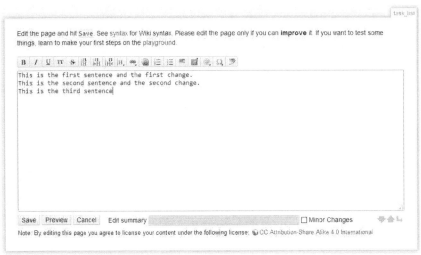

Figure 4. *The pink edit summary textbox.*

The second purpose is to remind you to enter a note about what you are changing, as shown in **Figure 5**.

Figure 5. *Adding a note to the Edit summary.*

When a visitor clicks the "Old revisions" button in the toolbar on the right side of the page, a list of changes made to the page, including the user who made the change and the date/time the change was made, is displayed. See **Figure 6**.

Figure 6. *Old revisions to the current page, complete with edit summary comments.*

As you can see in Figure 6, the text entered in the "Edit summary" box is displayed alongside that data if that text exists. (The bottom two revisions in the list were saved without any description entered in the "Edit Summary" edit box.) Thus, it's a good idea to enter a description of the change, and the change of color of the textbox to pink serves as a visual reminder.

Old Revisions vs Recent Changes

Chapter 5 pointed out the Recent Changes link in the upper right of the page. You may be wondering what the difference between that and the Old Revisions button is. Old Revisions displays changes to the current page, while Recent Changes displays a list of pages that have been changed, as shown in **Figure 7**.

Figure 7. *Recent Changes is a list of all pages that have been changed recently.*

Click on the page name to the page in question, and then click the Old Revisions button to see the changes on that page.

Hentzenwerke Publishing, Inc.
books@hentzenwerke.com • www.hentzenwerke.com

Using the basic formatting buttons on the toolbar

The buttons above the edit box (see **Figure 8**) perform functions such as formatting text, inserting elements into the page, and other actions. (If the buttons don't show up for you, see the **faq:toolbar** topic on the DokuWiki wiki.)

Figure 8. *Buttons to format text and perform other functions.*

Let's use a couple buttons to modify some text and then see how to preview it. But first we'll see what they do under the hood. The first five buttons on the left provide bold, italic, underline, monospace and strike-through formatting. The buttons insert meta-characters specific to a type of formatting into the edit box. These meta-characters, also called markup syntax or just syntax, are then converted by DokuWiki to display as the desired format in the resulting Web page. For example, to bold a string of text, enclose the string with two asterisks like so:

```
**very bold**
```

to create this:

very bold

The buttons simply take care of inserting the meta-characters instead of requiring you to remember the meta-characters yourself.

You can use the buttons two different ways. If you highlight a block of text (see **Figure 9**) and then click a button, the formatting will be applied to the highlighted text. See **Figure 10**.

Figure 9. *Highlighting a string of text about to be formatted.*

Figure 10. *The characters used to control bold formatting, displayed in the edit box.*

The results are shown in **Figure 11**.

Hentzenwerke Publishing, Inc.
books@hentzenwerke.com • www.hentzenwerke.com

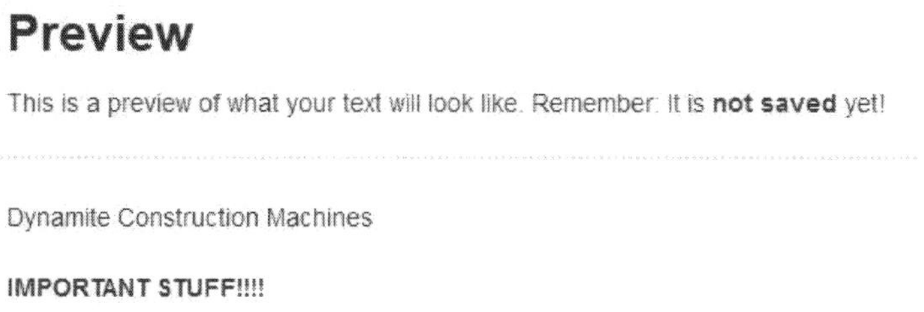
Preview
This is a preview of what your text will look like. Remember: It is not saved yet!
Dynamite Construction Machines
IMPORTANT STUFF!!!!

***Figure 11**. The result of formatting a string of text.*

Alternately, if you simply click a button after positioning your cursor somewhere in the editing box (**Figure 12**), a pre-formatted placeholder string (such as **Bold Text**) will be entered at the cursor. See **Figure 13**.

Dynamite Construction Machines
This is the less important stuff.
Save
Preview
Cancel
Edit summary
Minor Changes

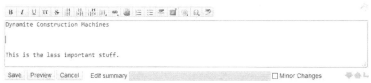

***Figure 12**. Position the cursor where you want a formatted placeholder.*

Dynamite Construction Machines
Bold Text
This is the less important stuff.
Save
Preview
Cancel
Edit summary
Minor Changes

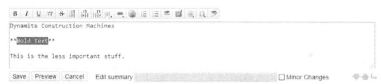

***Figure 13**. Click a formatting button and a formatted placeholder will be inserted.*

Now that you've got some formatted text on the page, you can use the "Preview" button under the box to see what the page will look like as shown in **Figure 14**.

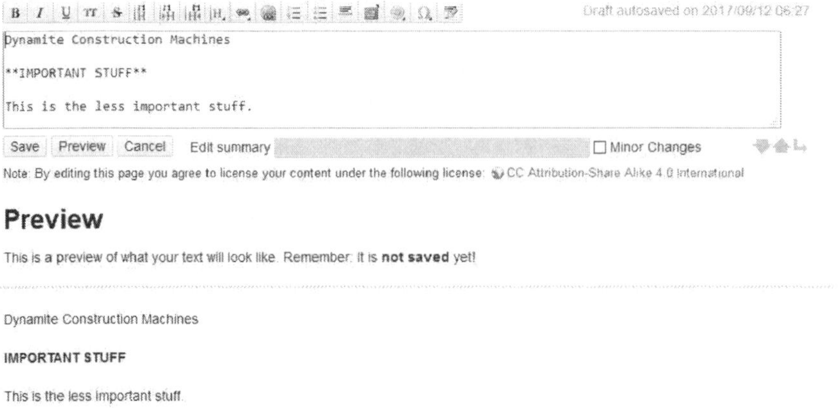

Figure 14. *A page being previewed.*

Note that when you're in preview mode, the preview display shows up **below** the editing box and the Save/Preview/Cancel buttons.

If you're happy with the page, click Save, else, make changes and Preview again, or just Cancel and go do something else until the muse hits you.

Monospaced text

While bold, italic, underline and strike-through are all common enough, the meaning of the 'monospaced text' button (with the 'TT' icon) may not be as obvious. It means to format the indicated text as 'code' – such as code in a software program. The reason this format is different than the rest is that regular text is formatted with a proportional, sans serif font. Program code, obviously, doesn't display well with such a font. Instead, program code is displayed in a fixed serif font, hence monospace. See **Figure 15**.

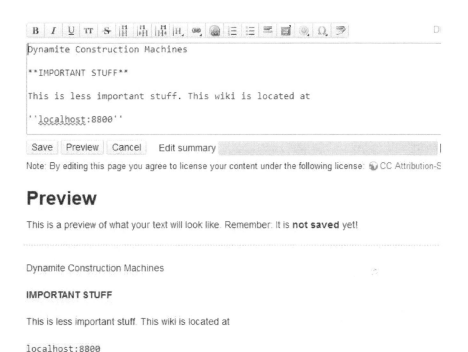

Preview

This is a preview of what your text will look like. Remember: It is **not saved** yet!

Dynamite Construction Machines

IMPORTANT STUFF

This is less important stuff. This wiki is located at

```
localhost:8800
```

Figure 15. *Using the 'code' marker for lines of code.*

Depending on your usage, you may run into a problem with this format - it's great for short snippets but what if you've got a bunch of code? See the 'Source code-specific features' section later in this chapter for a number of options.

H buttons

The next four buttons, labeled with variations of the capital letter H, format a string of text as a heading. The first H creates a heading the same level as the previous heading. The next two create a heading one level lower and one level higher, respectively. The fourth H button opens a second set of buttons, H1 through H5, that allow you to explicitly select which level heading. The meta-characters are simply a string of equal signs before and after the heading, as shown in **Figure 16**.

```
B  I  U  TT  ✄  ▯  ▯▯  ▯▯  H₁  ⚹  ◉  ☰  ☰  ☰  ☰  ◙  ▨  Ω  ➦        Draft autosaved on 2017/09/12 06:41

Dynamite Construction Machines                                                                      ^

====== Level 1 ======

===== Level 2 =====

==== Level 3 ====                                                                                   ⌄
```

Save   Preview   Cancel   Edit summary   ☐ Minor Changes   ⬇ ⬆ ⬑

Note: By editing this page you agree to license your content under the following license: ⚲ CC Attribution-Share Alike 4.0 International

Preview

This is a preview of what your text will look like. Remember: It is **not saved** yet!

....

Dynamite Construction Machines

Level 1

Level 2

Level 3

Table of Contents
● Level 1
◦ Level 2
◦ Level 3

Figure 16. Headings are formatted with equal signs as meta characters.

The contents of the "Table of Contents" box in the upper right is automatically generated using these headings. For consistency in the look of your pages and proper indentation of the Table of Contents, you shouldn't skip heading levels when adding content to a page. Start each page with an H1 and use subsequent H1 headlines to organize the content of a page into major sections. The next headings (H2, H3, etc.) should be used to break the major sections down into subsections.

There are two configuration settings - both found in the "Display Settings" section of the Configuration Manager - that affect headings. The "Top level for table of contents" setting controls which heading level begins a table of contents; by default it's set to '1'. I haven't found a need to change it to a different level. The "Maximum level for table of contents", set to '3' by default, controls how many levels are displayed in the table of contents box.

If you have a number of long pages with many nested levels, you may find that a setting of '3' is too busy - those pages will have too many sub-headings in the list - and choosing '2' is more to your liking. On the other hand, a wiki where most pages have just a couple of top levels but a lot of deeply nested content may benefit from a value of '4' or '5'.

Links

There are two link buttons in the toolbar - one for internal links and another for external links - but if you've tried them out, they appear to do the same thing - surround a string with double open and close square brackets, turning the string into a link. I've found they're both usually unnecessary, for different reasons, but exist as an easy reminder of what the differing syntaxes looks like.

DokuWiki is smart enough to automatically recognize external links, both for Web site addresses and email addresses. The one time you might want to use the

External Link button is when you want to use a linkname (instead of saying "The instructions are found at www.example.com and updates are at www.example.org", you might simply want to say "The instructions are here", where 'here' is a hyperlink to www.example.com.) For example, enter

```
Examples are http://www.example.com|here.
```

highlight the URL and phrase after the pipe. Then click the External Link button. The highlighted string gets converted like so:

```
Examples are [[http://www.example.com|here]].
```

And the result will display 'here' as a hyperlink to www.example.com. See **Figure 17.**

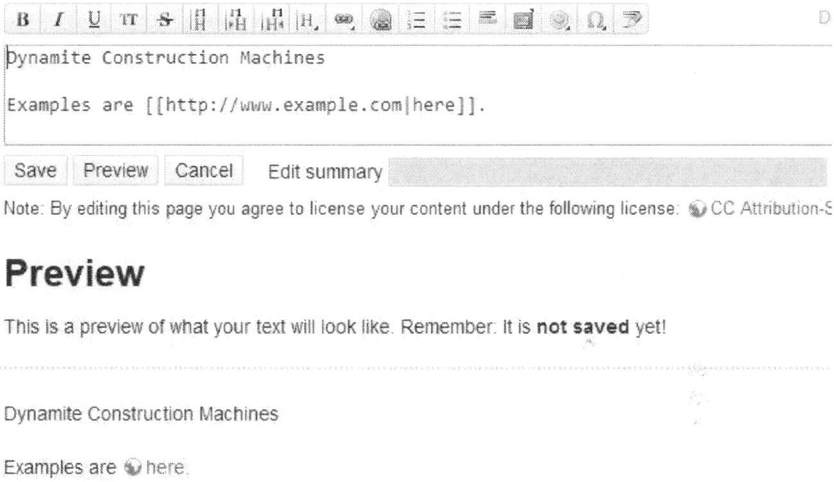

Figure 17. Various hyperlink options.

For internal links, I find that I'm usually typing the name of the internal page anyway, so it's no trouble to simply include the '[[' and ']]' before and after, which will turn the string into a link upon save. Internal link pops up a search window that matches partial text to page names (sort of like auto-complete), so you can see 'sandwiches', 'sidebar', and 'soforth' as soon as you type 's'.

Email addresses are also automatically recognized and turned into 'mail me' links, as long as you surround the string with less-than and greater-than signs. You can use the External Link button to use a linkname with an email address as well - in that case, lose the less-than/greater-than signs and place the linkname after the email address, separated by a pipe just like a URL:

```
Email me [[whil@whilhentzen.com|here]] or forever hold your peace.
```

There is a setting in the Configuration Manager that controls how email addresses are actually encoded on the Web page. See Chapter 8 for details.

Summary of link syntax

Internal pagename: [[Internal Specifications]]
URL: www.example.com
URL: http://www.example.com
URL with different label: [[http://www.example.com|Boring Website]]
Email address: Email me [[bob@example.com|here]].

Lists

There are two types of lists - unordered (or bulleted) and numbered, and they each do what they say. The meta-character for unordered lists is two spaces, an asterisk sign, and another space, while numbered lists use minus signs. Note that the two leading spaces are a required part of the meta-character string. See **Figure 18**.

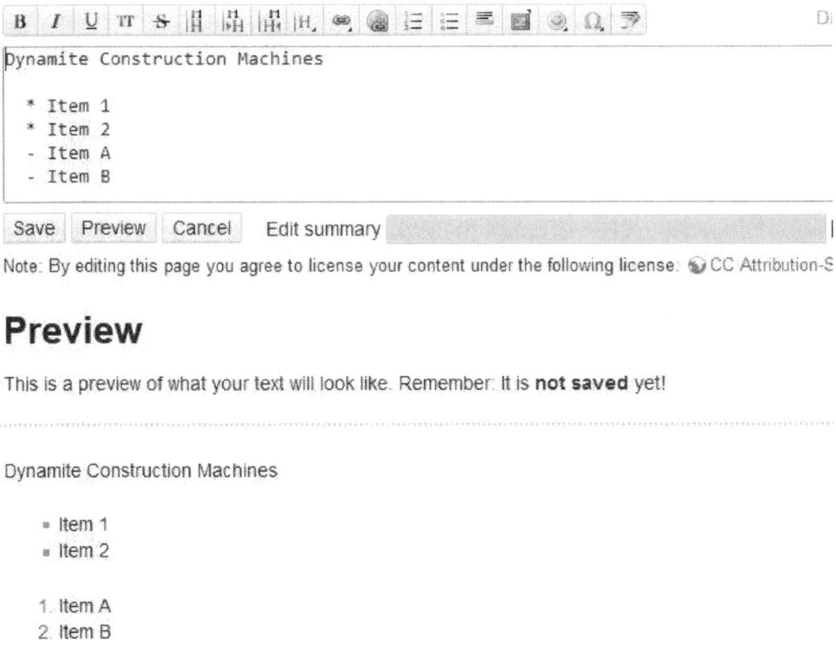

Figure 18. Formatting bulleted and numbered lists.

You'll notice in Figure 18 that the items are not separated by blank lines or by the '\\' line break meta-character. DokuWiki will automatically put each item on their own line. If you put a blank line between two items in a numbered list, the numbering will start all over again. A '\\' line break after an item in a numbered list will be ignored.

You can highlight a column list you've typed in and then click one of the list buttons to turn it into a list.

Insert objects

The last five buttons on the toolbar (we've been going left to right, if you haven't been paying attention) are used for inserting objects of one type or another. The objects (with the description of the icon) are:

```
Horizontal rule (blue line below greeked text)
Images (picture frame)
Smileys (yellow happy face)
Special characters (looks like a horseshoe, actually a lowercase
'omega' character)
Insert Signature (a blue pencil, only available when logged in)
```

I'll address each in their own section.

Horizontal Rule

The Horizontal Rule meta-character is simply four hyphens in a row on their own line. See **Figure 19**.

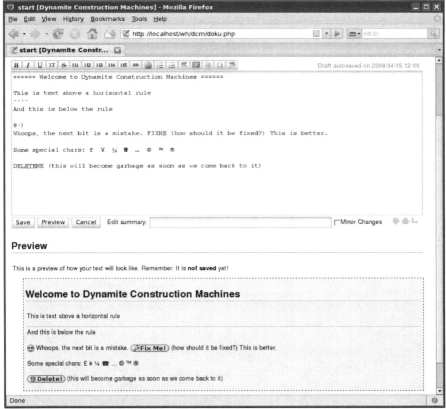

***Figure 19**. Displaying various objects.*

Smileys and Special Characters

The Smileys and Special Characters operate similarly. Click on the toolbar button and a box showing available choices displays. Click on a smiley or special character; the box will disappear and the character will be inserted into the page. Note that each smiley and special character has their own meta-character string - if you use one a great deal, you may find it faster to become acquainted with what that meta-character string is and just type it. (Generally, special characters are just hard-to-type UTF-8 characters which are inserted 'as-is'.)

If you've clicked on one of the toolbar buttons and then found you changed your mind, just clicking outside the box doesn't make it go away like for a tooltip. Instead, click on the toolbar button again to 'turn off' the display of the box.

There are two special smileys - FIXME and DELETE! - that deserve special mention. They both insert a bright yellow icon in the page that serves as a visual alert that the page needs work of some sort. The meta-characters are simply "FIXME" and "DELETEME" in all caps and jammed together.

Particularly during the development of a software specification, I've found that I have FIXME icons all over the place - so I've learned to type them rather than take my hands off the keyboard in order to mouse up to the toolbar.

A convention that I've found handy is to include the item to be fixed in parens immediately after the FIXME icon, like so:

```
FIXME (what is the default setting if there is more than one setting
available?)
```

Otherwise, it can be unclear later just what needs to be fixed - something before the alert, or after? And what span of text does the FIXME apply to? With a demarcation like parens, it's more obvious what I was referring to when I marked the text.

You can add your own smileys and special characters to the existing list. This is explained in Chapter 9.

Images and other files

You can add images to a wiki page via the "Add images and other files" button. While not difficult, the process has a couple of twists to it, so I'll walk through every step explicitly.

1. Go to a page where you want to add a picture.

2. Click "Edit this page".

3. Navigate to and place your cursor at the location in the page where you want the picture to be.

4. Click the "Images and other files" icon in the toolbar directly above the editing window. (It looks like a brown picture frame with a green something or other inside it, to the left of the yellow smiley face.)

5. A new "Media Files" dialog appears, as shown in **Figure 20**.

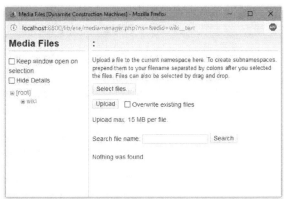

Figure 20. Getting ready to upload a media file.

6. Click the "Select files..." button.

7. A "Select file" dialog will appear.

8. Navigate to the photo on your local computer, highlight the file name, and select the "Open" button.

9. You'll be returned to the Media Files dialog.

10. The name (and path) of the file you selected will be displayed below the Select files... button. See **Figure 21.**

Figure 21. The name of the selected file is displayed below the button.

11. Click the "Upload" button.

12. After the file is uploaded from your local machine to the server hosting the wiki, the filename is displayed. See **Figure 22.**

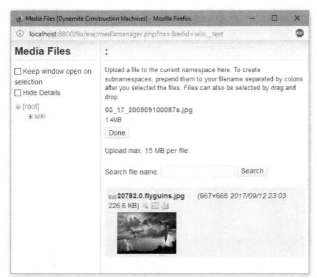

Figure 22. The name of the file after being uploaded.

12. Click the name of the file in bold, and Link Settings dialog will be displayed, giving you the option to specify how the image will display on the page. See **Figure 23**.

Figure 23. The Link Settings dialog.

Here you can specify how the target will look, how the image will be aligned, and what size the image will be. Once you make your choices, the link will be inserted in the wiki's edit page, as shown in **Figure 24**.

```
Dynamite Construction Machines

{{::03_17_200509100087s.jpg?400|}}
```

Save   Preview   Cancel   Edit summary

Figure 24. *The resulting link in the edit box.*

You'll notice the name of the file followed by a question mark and a numeric parameter, something like this:

`{{::03_17_200509100087s.jpg?400|}}`

13. Hit "Save" (or "Preview", if you're nervous) and you're all set. See **Figure 25**.

Figure 25. *These are Dynamite Construction Machines.*

Unless you're particularly lucky, you will probably want to make some changes. Most typically, you've just uploaded a gigantic (or minuscule) picture, and now the image is all out of proportion to the rest of the page. There are a couple of ways to fix this.

One choice would be resize the original image and upload it again. If you do so, but keep the same file name, note that you'll have to check the "Overwrite" checkbox after step 10. If you use a different filename, then the original image file will still be on the server that is hosting the DokuWiki site. You may want to get rid of it, just to keep things tidy.

Another choice is to incorporate additional parameters in the image link string to resize the image on the Web page. For example, suppose the original image is 1704x1392. This size will crowd out everything else on even the biggest Web pages. A more manageable size would be 340x278.

Include the resize parameter in the link to the image like so:

```
{{200509100087s.jpg?340x278}}
```

DokuWiki will resize the image on the server using the libGC or imagemagick library as selected in the Configuration Manager. If both are unavailable, using the resizing parms in the Web page may not be as good an option as actually resizing the image itself and uploading it again. If the original image is huge and you are shrinking it, visitors will end up downloading a file that's much bigger than it needs to be, chewing up bandwidth and precious disk space (OK, so disk space isn't that precious anymore, is it?), and increasing load time of the page. On the other hand, if the original image is very small, resizing it to make it bigger will likely just produce a pixelated image that doesn't look very good either.

There are oodles of handy options to tailor the display of the image once it's been loaded into the page. Including a string of text after the pipe ("|") character in the link like so:

```
{{::03_17_200509100087s.jpg?340x278|This tire won't ever go flat!}}
```

will cause that text to display as a tool tip. Inserting a space before the filename, like so:

```
{{ ::03_17_200509100087s.jpg?340x278|This tire won't ever go flat!}}
```

will cause the image to be right-aligned. **Figure 26** shows both effects.

Figure 26. *Right-aligning an image with a tool-tip.*

Similarly, including a space after the file name (and any size attributes that follow it) cause the image to be left aligned.

```
{{200509100087s.jpg?340x278 |This tire won't ever go flat!}}
```

Including a space before and after will center the image:

```
{{ 200509100087s.jpg?340x278 |This tire won't ever go flat!}}
```

You can just give the width of the desired output image, like so:

```
{{ 200509100087s.jpg?400 |This tire won't ever go flat!}}
```

and DokuWiki will automatically calculate the height necessary in order to maintain the aspect ratio of the picture.

Signatures

Since a wiki can be (and usually is) edited by multiple people, it can get confusing ('impossible') to determine who said what. You can add a link that contains the user's name as well as the date and time of the edit. This link is called a signature, and is inserted at the cursor's location by clicking the Signature button.

The format of the signature string defaults to the user's email address, their name, and the date/time. This definition can be changed in the Configuration Manager's Signature setting in the Display Settings block.

```
--- //[[@MAIL@|@NAME@]] @DATE@//
```

You are free to enter your own form of signature manually, just precede it with the following marker:

```
--- //your signature here
```

Where do you get these secret codes, such as @MAIL@ or @NAME@? See the 'Signature' setting in Chapter 8.

Signatures are only available if the wiki has been configured with ACL enabled and set to Public or Closed, since the system has no way of knowing who the user if logins aren't required (as is the case with no ACL or Open wikis.) Notice that the button itself disappears in those cases.

Signatures are most useful when you have a discussion style page, but you may also want to use them in order to specify who made what changes to a particular specification.

Advanced formatting

DokuWiki supports additional formatting features that are not available on the toolbar.

Footnotes

A footnote is a number placed in a paragraph that points to a reference at the bottom of the page. These can be a real pain to do manually; DokuWiki makes it easy. Almost too easy.

To create a footnote, just include the reference in a pair of double parens, like so:

```
There are hundreds of construction machines ((Journal of Construction
Machines, April, 2006)) in current use.
```

This results in a footnote marker in the text and the footnote, together with the number, being generated at the bottom of the page, as shown in **Figure 27**.

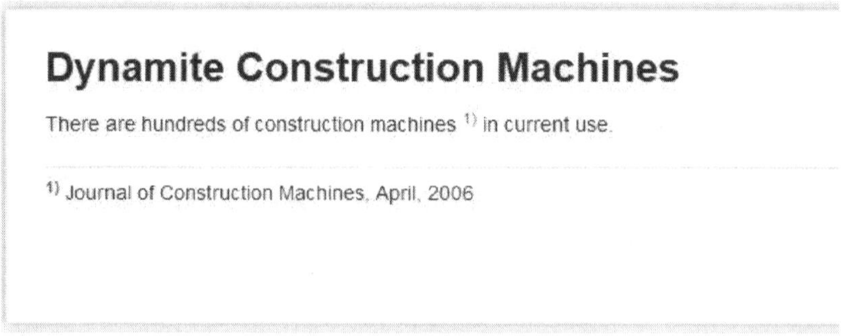

Dynamite Construction Machines

There are hundreds of construction machines [1] in current use.

[1] Journal of Construction Machines, April, 2006

Figure 27. Using double-parens to mark a footnote.

The academics among you will start 'ooo-ing' and 'aaah-ing' right now, as you see that you don't have to track the numbers - DokuWiki does it automatically for you. If you insert a third footnote between the two already in the text, DokuWiki will take care of renumbering. Wow. Good stuff, eh?

Typography

Just like the DokuWiki editor will format strings surrounded by meta-characters and convert certain character strings into smileys or other images, it will convert special typographical strings to their correct appearance. For example, typing

```
(c)   (r)   (tm)
```

will result in the display of

©   ®   ™

(These characters are also available with the Special characters button in the toolbar.)

This feature is also available for typographically correct single and double quotes. You can turn the quoting conversion on and off via the "Do typographical replacements" setting in the "Display settings" section in the Configuration Manager.

Quoting

Email clients have a feature that displays the back-and-forth nature of a series of emails so the reader can track who said what. DokuWiki has the same ability to mark pieces of a page as parts of a conversation. Use multiple instances of the greater-than sign (">") to indicate the various parties in a discussion. Entering text like this:

```
> > We need to add details about the machine upgrade.
>> Sales has decided to quote the upgrade separately.
> We still need to determine which upgrades are available.
>> Sales said they'll provide basic machine data by
>> the end of the week..
```

results in the display on the page shown in **Figure 28**.

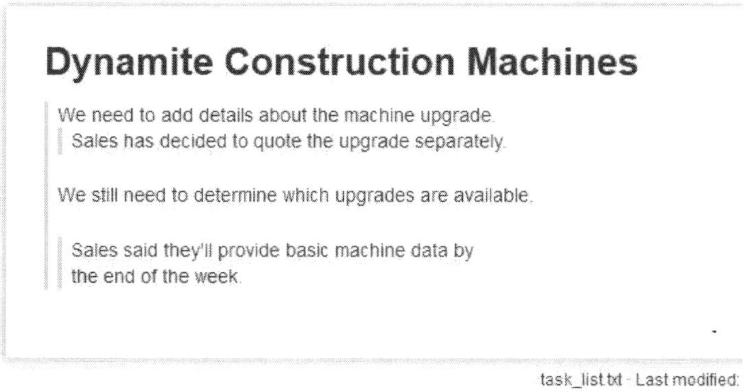

task_list.txt · Last modified:

Figure 28. Incorporating quoting in a page.

Use multiple greater-than signs (">>>>") to indicate deeper levels to the conversation.

Tables

While Web design purists may dismiss HTML tables as oh-so-five-minutes-ago (preferring to use mechanisms like CSS - Cascading Style Sheets - to control styling), they're still an easy and useful way to organize information in single Web pages - and they're a lot easier for the casual user to work with than trying to encapsulate CSS into a meta-language. The results of the following examples are all displayed in **Figure 29**.

The meta-character for defining tables is the pipe ("|"). Here's a simple table:

```
| Who | Section | Due Date |
```

Horizontal and Vertical Headers

If you want to set off the table headers, use the caret ("^") instead of the pipe for the header row:

```
^ Who ^ Section ^ Due Date ^
| Al | T of C | 4/16 |
```

Use the caret on the left side of cells to create a vertical header:

```
^ Who ^ Section ^ Due Date ^
^ Al | T of C | 4/16 |
^ Bob | Intro | 4/20 |
```

Text alignment

The contents of cells can be aligned individually, using two or more spaces on the end of the text opposite where you want the alignment to occur. For example, to right-align the contents of a cell (say, for numbers or currency amounts), put two or more spaces in front of the string. To center the contents of a cell, use two or more spaces on both sides of the string. The following example shows the Due Date centered and the the Budget aligned to the right.

```
^ Who ^ Section ^  Due Date  ^ Budget ^
^ Al | T of C |   4/16   |  $21,150.00 |
^ Bob | Intro |   4/20   |  $922.75 |
```

Spanning cells

You can also have individual cells span multiple columns:

```
^ Who ^ Section ^ Due Date ^
| Al | T of C | 4/16 |
| Bob | Intro | 4/20 |
| Carol | Index (mult)| |
| Donna (gone)|| till 5/1|
```

In each of these examples, I put a single space before and after the contents purely for readability's sake.

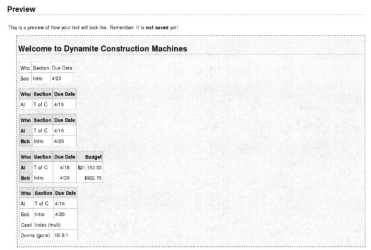

Figure 29. Examples of various table features.

As you can see, formatting a table in DokuWiki is simple to the point of being trivial - sure beats trying to encode the nuances of HTML and CSS!

Source code-specific features

DokuWiki has a boatload of features that are of specific help to software jocks working on documentation. These include the inclusion of source code in a wiki page, dealing with HTML and PHP code snippets in a wiki page, syntax highlighting of a block of source code (DokuWiki supports dozens of languages), and tagging blocks of text to be ignored by the parsing engine (non-parsed blocks). Let's look at each of these.

Embedding source code

We're programmers. We write code. And we want to show off our code to the world. Or at least that part of the world who has access to our wiki. However, the default font for wiki pages is a proportional one, which does not bode well for displaying readable source code.

We saw the 'code text' button earlier in this chapter, but it has one significant problem - multiple lines must be flagged with a newline ("\\") character to prevent the code from wrapping onto a single line. Ugly and tedious if you have more than a couple of lines of code.

Surrounding a block of text (that spans multiple lines) with <code> and </code> tags formats source code that way you would want it to look - with a mono-spaced font and a colored background to set it off from the text before and after it.

```
<code>
    * a very sophisticated loop
    for i = 1 to n
      print i, i^2
    next
</code>
```

Surrounding a block of text with the <file> and </file> tags does the same thing, except with a contrasting color for the background.

```
<file>
    * a very sophisticated loop
    for i = 1 to n
      print i, i^2
    next
</file>
```

Figure 30 shows blocks of text surrounded by the <code> and the <file> tags.

Preview

This is a preview of how your text will look like. Remember: It is **not saved** yet!

```
Welcome to Dynamite Construction Machines

Using <code>

    * a very sophisticated loop
    for i = 1 to 10
       print i
    next

Using <file>

    * an even more  sophisticated loop
    n = 101
    for i = 1 to n step 2
       print i, i^2
    next
```

Figure 30. *Using <code> and <file> tags to separate source code from the rest of a page.*

There are additional tags you can use to alter the way a block of text is parsed; see the 'Non-parsed blocks' section later in this chapter.

Embedding HTML and PHP

Because DokuWiki is built with PHP and renders HTML, displaying HTML and PHP code requires a bit of special handling. First, note that HTML and PHP code in a wiki page are not automatically parsed and executed, because doing so blindly is a security risk. Enabling HTML will allow XSS (Cross Site Scripting) attacks, while enabling PHP allows a malevolent user to run their own code on your server - as Andi notes, "it just screams 'root my server'!"

If you have a particular scenario where you absolutely, positively need these capabilities, such as on an Intranet with a limited number of users, you *might* consider using the "Allow embedded HTML" and "Allow embedded PHP" settings in the "Editing Settings" section of the Configuration Manager allow this default to be changed. See Chapter 7 for details.

Once the configuration setting is changed, using <html> and </html> tags around a block of HTML code will cause it to work as if it were part of the page's regular HTML. The following code displays as shown in **Figure 31**.

```
<html>
Machines are great to <span style="color:red;">own</span> or <span
style="color:green;">rent</span>.
</html>
```

```
<html>
<p style="border:2px dashed red;">
Machines are great to <span style="color:red;">own</span> or <span
style="color:green;">rent</span>
</p>
</html>
```

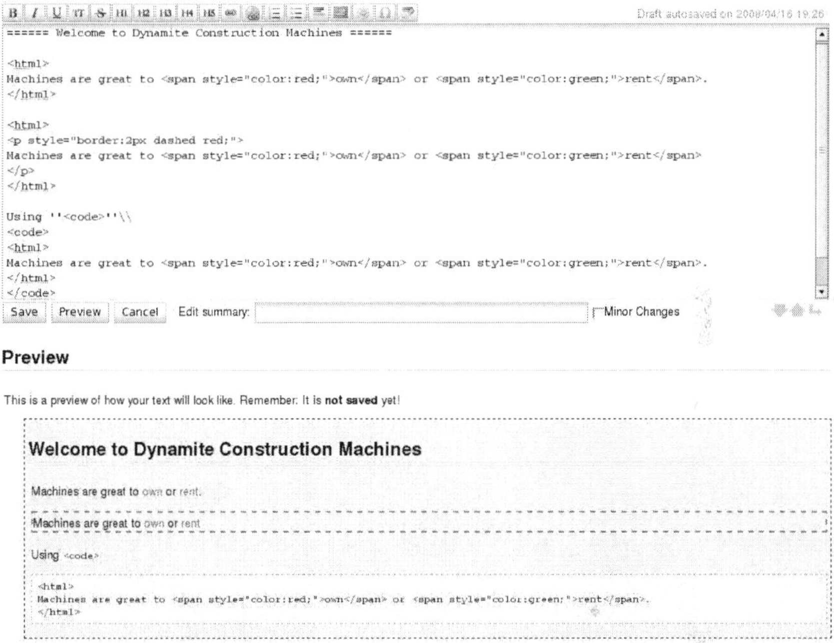

Figure 31. Embedding HTML in a DokuWiki Web page.

By way of contrast, the following code, using the <code> tag and shown in the bottom of Figure 27, displays the <html> tags and doesn't interpret the HTML:

```
Using ''<code>''\\
<code>
<html>
This is some <span style="color:red;font-size:150%;">inline HTML</span>
</html>
</code>
```

Similarly, the <php> and </php> tags operate on PHP code as long as the "Allow embedded PHP" setting in the Configuration Manager is checked. For example, the following code

```
<php>
phpinfo();
```

```
</php>
```

results in the display shown in **Figure 32**.

Figure 32. *Embedding PHP code in a DokuWiki Web page.*

It's probably a good idea again to remind you that enabling embedded PHP is a huge security risk unless your wiki is tightly restricted.

Syntax highlighting

Most modern editors automatically display source code with syntax highlighting - keywords in one color, constants in a second, variables in a third, and so on. And many a programmer has been thrilled when their weapon of choice was added to the list of languages automatically detected by the editor. Why should DokuWiki be any different?

DokuWiki uses GeSHi - Generic Syntax Highlighter - that's used by a number of software applications, including phpBB, Joomla and WakkaWiki. It's just a PHP script (a class, actually) that is included with DokuWiki.

Remember how you used <code> and </code> tags to mark a block of text as source code? You do the same thing with GeSHi, except that you need to include the name of the language in the tag. For example, if you're using that cool desktop database language that Microsoft has been trying to destroy for the last 15 years, you'd do this:

```
<code visualfoxpro>
use CUSTOMER order cNaL
seek 'DASTARDLY'
browse last
nAmount = CUSTOMER.nAmount * 1.15
</code>
```

resulting in the display shown in **Figure 33**.

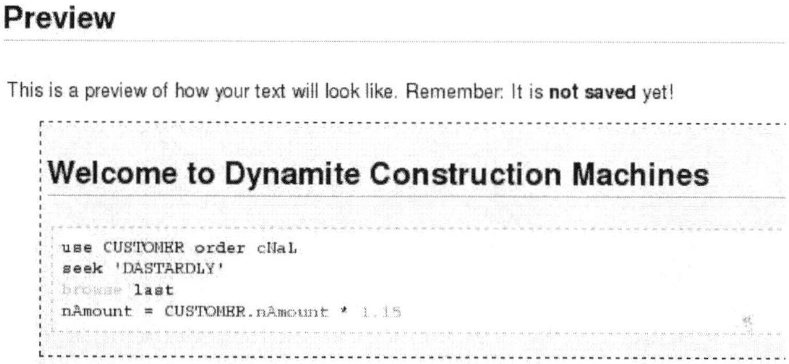

Preview

This is a preview of how your text will look like. Remember: It is **not saved** yet!

Welcome to Dynamite Construction Machines

```
use CUSTOMER order cNaL
seek 'DASTARDLY'
browse last
nAmount = CUSTOMER.nAmount * 1.15
```

Figure 33. Using GeSHI to apply syntax highlighting to Visual FoxPro code.

More about GeSHi

The GeSHi scripts that come with DokuWiki may be dated, depending on the version of DokuWiki that you're using. Your requirements may make it worthwhile to get the very latest GeSHi scripts.

You can grab the most recent GeSHi from their website, http://gbnz.com/highlighter. It comes compressed; download to your dw_masters folder and unzip it, creating a folder named 'geshi'. (I rename the folder to include the version number, so the folder is named geshi-1.0.7.21.)

You'll see a php script, geshi.php, and three sub-folders, contrib, docs, and geshi. "contrib" contains examples, "docs" contains documentation, a copy of the GPL license, and other information, and "geshi" contains separate PHP scripts for every language it supports. (There are nearly 90 languages in that list - really quite impressive.)

In order to incorporate more recent GeSHi scripts into your DokuWiki installation, copy the geshi.php file and the PHP files in the 'geshi' folder to 'inc' and 'inc/geshi' respectively and then load up DokuWiki again.

You can add line numbers via the code2 plugins and you can tailor the syntax coloring via modifications to the CSS.

Non-parsed blocks

Finally, you can indicate to DokuWiki that you want it to completely ignore a block of text, referred to as 'non-parsed blocks' (because you don't want the DokuWiki parser to do its magic on the block.)

There are a couple of ways to make this happen; which you use depends on how much text you want to deal with.

First is to simply indent every line of interest by two spaces. This is the cheap way out, not recommended except for a quick and dirty line or two.

The second way, much preferred, is to surround the block of text of interest with <nowiki> tags. (That's 'no wiki', not 'now iki' as one reviewer initially thought!) For example, using the code in the HTML example earlier:

```
<nowiki>
<html>
Machines are great to <span style="color:red;">own</span> or <span
style="color:green;">rent</span>.
</html>
</nowiki>
```

But why type all those characters - eight of them in "<nowiki>"? Use "%%" to bracket a block like this:

```
%%
<html>
Machines are great to <span style="color:red;">own</span> or <span
style="color:green;">rent</span>.
</html>
%%
```

to get the same effect. **Figure 34** shows the results.

```
B  I  U  TT  S  H1  H2  H3  H4  H5  ∞  ≣  ≡  ≣  🖼  Ω  ⌐          Draft autosaved on 2
====== Welcome to Dynamite Construction Machines ======

<nowiki>
<html>
Machines are great to <span style="color:red;">own</span> or <span style="color:green;">rent</span>.
</html>
</nowiki>

%%
<html>
Machines are great to <span style="color:red;">own</span> or <span style="color:green;">rent</span>.
</html>
%%

<html>
<p style="border:2px dashed red;">
Machines are great to <span style="color:red;">own</span> or <span style="color:green;">rent</span>
</p>
```

| Save | Preview | Cancel | Edit summary: [   ] | ☐ Minor Changes |

Preview

This is a preview of how your text will look like. Remember: It is **not saved** yet!

Welcome to Dynamite Construction Machines

<html> Machines are great to own or rent. </html>

<html> Machines are great to own or rent. </html>

Machines are great to own or rent

Using <code>

```
<html>
Machines are great to <span style="color:red;">own</span> or <span style="color:green;">rent</span>.
</html>
```

Figure 34. *Using '<nowiki>' and '%%' to prevent parsing of a block. (Note that HTML is enabled globally, which is why the 3rd paragraph renders.)*

An additional benefit to the "%%" construct is that this is also useful inline, like when you don't want a link to be clickable: %%http://www.example.com%%

Other goodies

DokuWiki has a couple of other editing and formatting features that just don't fit anywhere else. Here they are.

Control Macros (Controlling page rendering)

When DokuWiki renders a page, it automatically performs certain functions. Two of those are the generation of a Table of Contents and caching the copy of the page in the /data/attic/cache folder. You can restrict either of these behaviors by including specific text strings anywhere on the page. DokuWiki refers to these as 'control macros'.

Including

~~NOTOC~~

on a page, no table of contents will be created.
Similarly, including

```
~~NOCACHE~~
```

will prevent DokuWiki from caching the current page. This forces DokuWiki to
render the page anew each time it is displayed. While more intensive from a server
point of view, if the page has data in it that is dynamic in nature (e.g. a php script
that generates new results each time it's displayed), you may want to incorporate this
macro in the page.

Syntax Plugins
Plugins are modules that can be added to DokuWiki in order to extend (or modify)
its functionality. There are literally hundreds of plugins, and a great many of them
have to do with syntax. Plugins are covered in more detail in Chapter 11, Your First
Plugins.

Extending the button toolbar
Depending on your usage of DokuWiki, you may find yourself performing the same
formatting action(s) over and over. If you're comfortable with PHP, you may want to
try to extend the button toolbar yourself. There's an example of how this was done
for a print view button in the **tips:printview** topic. Additionally, as of this writing,
there's a placeholder in the tips section of the wiki (**tips:toolbarbutton**) for
generically adding toolbar buttons.

Spellchecking
Finally, the editor is spellchecker-aware. Right click on a word with a red squiggle
under it and the context menu you expect will display, as shown in **Figure 35**.

Figure 35. Spellchecking in the edit window.

Conclusion

In this chapter, I've covered just about every editing capability that exists in DokuWiki. The trick for you is to remember some of the rarer functions and format codes. To get started, right-click on the 'syntax' link at the top of every editing page and select "Open in New..." as shown in **Figure 36**.

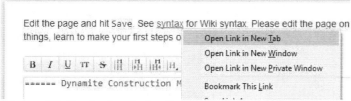

Figure 36. Navigating to the Doku Wiki's syntax help page.

Additionally, the online manual on the DokuWiki web site

`https://www.dokuwiki.org/manual`

is excellent.

10. Version Mania: Changes, Revision, Drafts and Stuff

Not only is DokuWiki a great wiki tool, but it acts as a poor man's version control system with mechanisms for saving drafts, handling changes to pages, and archiving old versions of pages. With this extended capability come some nuances that may not be completely obvious at first. In this chapter, we'll discuss how each of these functions works and what types of things you can do with them. In addition, we'll start to peer at what's happening under the hood.

This chapter covers four seemingly disparate topics that all are related under the surface. First and most importantly, allowing access to edit a page on the Web means that you're working with a multi-user system, which immediately injects all sorts of dynamics - regarding page locking - into an otherwise mundane operation of text editing. Then there are the variety of version handling functions - saving changes and old revisions. But before any of that, text editing itself opens up the issue of automatically saving drafts for the user. Let's begin.

By the way, the operation of many of these features can be tailored to your liking via settings in the DokuWiki Configuration Manager which is described in full detail in Chapter 8.

Draft saving

DokuWiki automatically saves a copy ("a draft") of the page being edited. On each keystroke, it is checked if the last saved draft is older than 30 seconds; if so, a new draft is saved. This file is called the 'draft file'. The draft file expires when a new revision of the page is saved.

In the event of a crash of a component of your system (say, a browser crash, or a Blue Screen of Death on Windows), return to the page that you were editing at the time. The "Edit" button will be replaced by a "Recover Draft" button when a draft is available. (A copy wouldn't be available if the crash occurred inside the 30 second window, or if the user's browser has JavaScript disabled. In other words, a maximum of 30 seconds of work will be lost.)

In order to force the saving of a draft, click the Preview button during editing.

This functionality can be turned off by unchecking the "Automatically save a draft while editing" setting in the "Editing Settings" section of the Configuration Manager.

Page locking

DokuWiki locks a page for a specific period of time (the 'locktime') when it is edited by a user. How does this work? Suppose Bill begins editing a page. Shortly

Hentzenwerke Publishing, Inc.
books@hentzenwerke.com • www.hentzenwerke.com

thereafter, Barb visits the page. Barb's Edit button is still enabled, but as soon as she clicks it, a warning (instead of the edit box) will be displayed, as shown in **Figure 1**.

Page locked

This page is currently locked for editing by another user. You have to wait until this user finishes editing or the lock expires.

* **Currently locked by:** bill
* **Lock expires at:** 2008/04/27 12:43 (15 min)

conventions_abbreviations.txt · Last modified 2008/03/14 18:34 by bill · Currently locked by bill   Back to top

Figure 1. *A second user is warned when they attempt to edit a page that is already being edited by the first user.*

The warning includes the name of who is editing the page (if available) as well as when the page will be available (although locks can be extended, or released early.) DokuWiki notifies the editing user that the lock is going to expire a minute in advance as shown in **Figure 2**.

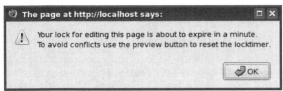

Figure 2. *Lock expiration warning.*

If the editing user ignores the warning, the lock is abandoned and another user can then edit the page.

The 'locktime' is configurable via the "Maximum age for lock files (sec)" setting in the Editing Settings section of the Configuration Manager. The value is in seconds, with a default of 900 (15 minutes.)

Conflict resolution with multiple pending edits

It's important to note that the goal of the lock is to prevent a second user from getting into edit mode. It is possible through a perfectly legitimate set of circumstances for two people to get into edit mode at the same time. Fortunately, DokuWiki has a second line of defense to prevent problems when this happens.

Suppose Al started editing the page, locking it. Then he walks away and doesn't see, or simply ignores, the 'The lock is about to expire' message. A minute passes. The lock is removed, and now that page is open for others to edit. However, he's still got an edit box open in his browser - *he's still in edit mode*!

Barb starts editing the page. Doing so issues a new lock, and no one can visit the page and click the Edit this page button. So when a third visitor, Chuck, visits the page and clicks "Edit this page", he gets the "Page locked" message shown back in Figure 1. So far, so good.

However, remember that Al was *already* in edit mode. Now suppose that, while Barb is editing madly, Al returns to his computer and continues his original editing as well. We've now got two people in edit mode - the very situation that we didn't want.

Now you can see how the lock prevents the next **new** visitor to the page from initiating an edit but it doesn't prevent a second user who had an edit window open from messing with the page in their already open window. This is because the editing is done in the browser on the client machine. So, what happens?

First, unlike some conflict resolution systems where the last man standing wins (the last person's edits overwrite the second last person's edits), with DokuWiki, whoever saves first wins. Back to our example - both Al and Barb have open edit windows. If Al adds a line and saves his edits, that's what the new page now looks like. Then, ten blimptoseconds later, when Barb adds her line and attempts to save, DokuWiki employs its second line of defense - the 'newer version exists' warning page as shown in **Figure 3**.

A newer version exists

A newer version of the document you edited exists. This happens when another user changed the document while you were editing it.

Examine the differences shown below thoroughly, then decide which version to keep. If you choose save, your version will be saved. Hit cancel to keep the current version.

Save   Cancel

conventions_abbreviations 2008/04/27 13.35current   Your Version

Figure 3. A "newer version exists" warning alerts the second user to save changes.

This page will warn the second user (Barb) that someone else (Al) has shortstopped the page and gotten their changes saved first. The differences between the two pages are also displayed in a color-coded side-by-side listing. The second user (Barb) is offered the choice of abandoning their edits or having their version overwrite the existing version on disk. If the second user (Barb) chooses to have their changes overwrite the existing page, the first user (Al) will be able to see the new page with the other user's (Barb's) changes when they click their Refresh button or navigate back to the page later, but their own changes will have been lost.

Interestingly enough, the non-obvious but significant win in this "Who Saves Last Wins" scenario is that both changes were recorded in Old Revisions, and can be recalled and manually merged if necessary. Nothing was lost in the overwriting.

Under the hood

If you poke around on disk while working with page locking, you'll see that DokuWiki creates a 'lock file' in the data/locks folder when a user edits a page. This file has a name like

```
ea2b2676c28c0db26d39331a336c6b92.lock
```

and contains either the username, if available, or the IP address of the client doing the editing. Using the username or IP ensures that you can't lock yourself out.

The lockfile is automatically deleted when the page is saved or the edits are canceled, or when locktime has expired. If a user hits Preview, the lockfile's expiration time is automatically reset to the current time plus the locktime. This means that the user can keep the page locked by using the Preview feature regularly. (DokuWiki notifies the user that the lock is about to expire in one minute.) Automatic Draft saving extends the lock as well, so you can write for hours without needing to press preview and your lock will be extended every 30 seconds.

Note that DokuWiki locks the entire page, even if the user clicks the Edit button for just a single section of that page.

Caching

Displaying a page on a wiki could potentially be sluggish due to the processing involved in turning a simple text file into the final product that the visitor to the page sees. DokuWiki avoids needless processing by caching pages that have already been parsed. As a result, a page that was recently parsed is stored for future recall. This collection of stored pages is called a cache. If a cached copy of a page is present in the data/cache folder, it is presented to the client browser for rendering instead of forcing the computer to parse the page again. This is true only for pages being viewed - pages in the process of being edited or previewed are parsed each time a new operation is executed.

There are actually two stages to the caching process, as explained in "Under the Hood" later in this section. The second stage is influenced by to the "Maximum age for cache (sec)" setting in the "Editing Settings" section of the Configuration Manager. The default is 86,400 seconds, or one day.

Force a refresh

While the cache is generally a good thing, there can be times that you don't want to use the cached copy, but instead need the page to be parsed anew. To do so manually, include the "purge=true" clause to a URL. If the URL doesn't have already have a clause with a "?" delimiter, use this syntax:

```
http://localhost/wh/dcm/doku.php?purge=true
```

while if there already is a ?-delimited clause, use the "&" to add the second clause:

Hentzenwerke Publishing, Inc.
books@hentzenwerke.com • www.hentzenwerke.com

```
http://localhost/wh/dcm/doku.php?id=start&purge=true
```

Changing the timestamp of the conf/local.php file (done via 'touch' in Linux) will force recaching all pages in the wiki.

Prevent caching all the time

There are occasions that a page should be parsed each time it is viewed, such as when it has dynamic content that should be evaluated for each visitor. Including the

```
~~NOCACHE~~
```

control macro in the page will force the page to be parsed each time.

It's probably a good idea (if not a Best Practice) to put the ~~NOCACHE~~ tag at the top of the page as a reminder; if it's down near the bottom, out of sight, the next editor of the page might unnecessarily add a second copy of the tag - and then wonder why the page isn't being cached after they remove their copy of the tag.

Images

Just as parsing pages on every request can be a drag on the server, reading images from disk on every view can produce a significant performance problem. For this reason, DokuWiki also caches external images by default.

If, for some reason, you need to link to an external image and dynamically load it each view (say, a weather widget that auto-updates), add the "nocache" parameter to the link, like so:

```
{{http://www.example.net/images/an_important_image.png?nocache}}
```

Use the "&" separator if you are using an image-oriented parameter string that has already used up the "?" parameter. The following link includes a resizing parameter:

```
{{http://www.example.net/images/an_important_image.png?
100x200&nocache}}
```

Obviously, you don't want to dynamically load external images on every view. At the same time, if you don't force a reload, the image in the cache will stay there indefinitely. You can achieve a middle ground, forcing the external image to be reloaded based on the frequency that pages are reloaded, through the "recache" parameter:

```
{{http://www.example.net/images/an_important_image.png?recache}}
```

This will force DokuWiki to reload (and then cache) the external image using the loadtime value in the Configuration Manager.

Hentzenwerke Publishing, Inc.
books@hentzenwerke.com • www.hentzenwerke.com

Under the hood

Cache files are stored in /cache. However, if you've looked in data/cache, you'll see a folder structure considerably more complex than, say, the files in data/locks.

First of all, there are multiple folders, each consisting of a single letter, under data/cache. The MD5 sum of certain multiple data (like pagename and hostname) identifies a piece of cached information uniquely. For faster access the cachefiles are sorted into directories matching their first letter. The page's path + file name is hashed and the cache file is filed under the folder matching the first character of the name hash. The structure of the cache folder is simple: the first letter of the hash of the page gives the folder in which the page is stored.

In these folders are at least two files per cached page. The first file has an 'i' extension, and represents the results of an intermediate processing step - the results after instructions (such as applying tags) have been parsed, but before the page is rendered into XHTML. This is used by the indexer. The second file ends in .xhtml, and is the final result (the rendered page) passed to the browser.

A third page, with a .js extension, contains the Javascript of the page. If needed there is also a code part of the page (.code) and css part (.css).

The instruction cache file gets updated only when any of four specific files are changed:

- The page itself
- Either of two config files (conf/dokuwiki.php and conf/local.php)
- Either of two core DokuWiki PHP files (inc/parser/parser.php & inc/parser/handler.php) are changed
- Any plugins are added or enabled, or removed or disabled - using the plugin manager.

The final XHTML cache file is updated when the instruction cache file is updated and also in several more situations:

- When the cachetime setting expires
- Its metadata, such as the time last updated, who last updated the page, and so on. And plugins can add additional metadata. When the metadata changes the HTML is re-rendered.
- Either of two more core DokuWiki PHP files (inc/parser/xhtml & inc/parser/metadata) are changed,
- When the link target page is changed (created or deleted), and
- When an RSS feed needs to be refreshed.

Generally, this level of detail will be useful only when you are creating templates or plugins that will have an effect on a page.

Cache and Revisions Eraser plugin

Finally, you might find it useful to be able to clear the cache, perhaps if it gets corrupted or if you're experiencing unusual problems that might be cache-related.

The Cache and Revisions Eraser plugins will allow you to erase the entire cache. Plugins are covered in more detail in Chapter 12, Your First Plugins.

Old revisions

Each wiki page has an "Old revisions" button. Clicking this button will display a list of instances when changes made to the current page were saved.

This list is particularly helpful when the folks who made the edits included comments in the "Edit summary" text box under the edit box before saving their edits, as the list of changes includes the information entered in the "Edit summary" text box. See **Figure 4**.

Old Revisions

These are the older revisons of the current document. To revert to an old revision, select it from below, click Edit this page and save it.

■ ☐ *2008/06/04 10:58*   technical_specifications – *(current)*
■ ☐ *2008/06/04 10:58* 👓 technical_specifications –
■ ☐ 2008/06/04 10:56 👓 technical_specifications – added questions re os, hw
■ ☐ *2008/06/04 10:56* 👓 technical_specifications –
■ ☐ 2008/06/04 10:55 👓 technical_specifications – added summary
■ ☐ 2008/06/04 10:55 👓 technical_specifications – created with main sections

[Show differences between selected revisions]

***Figure 4**. The Old Revisions list allows a user to see earlier copies of a page.*

The first column is a checkbox that allows you to select a specific revision for comparing to another. The second column is, obviously, the date and time that the page was changed. The third either displays a pair of 3-D glasses with one blue lens and one red lens or a blank space. This icon is a shortcut to compare the page revision to the current version the page. In concert with the glasses icon is the name of the page in the fourth column. If it's a hyperlink (green), that's how you get to the copy of the old version; if it's not hyperlinked, then you're out of luck. (Why? See 'Under the Hood' later in this chapter.) The next column lists the comment entered in the "Edit summary" text box under the edit box during editing. The last column contains the name or IP address of the person who edited the page.

You can examine an old version simply by clicking the green link to the page. Doing so will display the page together with a warning, as shown in **Figure 5**.

This is an old revision of the document!

Technical Specifications

The Technical Specifications include four major sections. Questions still to be answered are included at the bottom of the page.

Environment
Data
Throughput Analysis
Architecture

Questions:

1. Operating systems supported?
2. Control over hardware?

Figure 5. *Viewing an old revision of the current page.*

You can restore an old version via the Load old, Edit and Save process.

You can compare revisions using a couple of different mechanisms. If you want to compare the current page with another page, click on the glasses icon (in Figure 4) next to the other page. The differences between that page and the current page will be displayed side by side, as shown in **Figure 6**.

Differences

This shows you the differences between the selected revision and the current version of the page.

technical_specifications 2008/06/04 10:58   technical_specifications 2008/06/04 10:58 current

Line 8:   Line 8:
 [[Technical Specifications:Architecture]]\\   [[Technical Specifications:Architecture]]\\
- **Questions:**   + **Questions**
 1. Operating systems supported?\\   1. Operating systems supported?\\
 2. Control over hardware?\\   2. Control over hardware?\\

Figure 6. *Use the glasses icon to view the differences between the current page and another page.*

You can also compare two older versions. Select the two pages of interest via the checkboxes on the far left (again, Figure 4) and then click the 'Show differences between selected revisions' button. See **Figure 7**.

Differences

This shows you the differences between the selected revision and the current version of the page.

technical_specifications 2008/06/04 10:55   technical_specifications 2008/06/04 10:58

Line 1:   Line 1:
                                               + The Technical Specifications include four major sections. Questions
                                                 still to be answered are included at the bottom of the page.
                                               +
 [[Technical Specifications:Environment]]\\   [[Technical Specifications:Environment]]\\
 [[Technical Specifications:Data]]\\   [[Technical Specifications:Data]]\\
Line 4:   Line 6:
 [[Technical Specifications:Architecture]]\\   [[Technical Specifications:Architecture]]\\
                                               + **Questions:**
                                               +
                                               +1. Operating systems supported?\\
                                               +2. Control over hardware?\\

Figure 7. *Viewing differences between two older pages.*

To get back to the original page from the 'Differences' list, click the 'Show page' button at the far left in either the top or bottom blue bar.

Under the hood

Each time a page is changed, the old version is copied to the /data/attic folder in compressed form. (You can choose the type of compression, including no compression, in the Configuration Manager.) These files are the ones used for display when the user clicks on an old page's name in the list. This explains why some files in the listing can be edited and others can't - the ones that don't have hyperlinks don't have their corresponding versions stored in the attic. (DokuWiki never deletes an old revision, so all revisions should be available. However, that doesn't mean that an old revision couldn't be removed manually.) You can test this out by temporarily moving one of those files with a .gz extension out of the attic and then refreshing the "Old Revisions" page.

You may be wondering how it is that the list contains versions of pages that no longer exist in the attic. It's because the "Old revisions" list for each page is stored as a separate file in the data/meta folder. For example, the 'start.changes' page is a text file containing the changes made to 'start'. When a page is modified, the '.changes' text file is updated. Thus, you can remove files from the attic but still have a list of changes that had been made to the file, sort of like having an address book that contains addresses of houses that have been demolished in order to make room for a shopping center.

Recent changes

The "Recent changes" button will display a list of up to the last 20 pages in the wiki that were changed, in a similar fashion to the "Old revisions" list, but without the checkbox. (The number 20 is configurable via the 'recent' configuration option.) The checkbox is gone because there will be many different pages in the list, and it wouldn't make sense to compare two different pages.

If there are more than 20 pages that have been changed, a "less recent >>" button will display underneath the list - sort of like a 'next 20' control. Clicking that button will display the next 20 (pages 21 through 40), and a second button, "<< more recent", that goes back to the first 20, will also be displayed.

The number of pages shown on a page can changed in the Configuration Manager via the "Recent Changes' setting in the 'Display Settings' section.

Note that this page will only list every page that has been changed, but not how many changes were made on each of those pages, nor each of the times that those pages were changed.

For instance, suppose you've got a 'start' page without much content. Bored, you decide to add a link to 'Test Page B', and then create Test Page B. Next, back on the 'start' page, you add a second link, this time to 'Test Page C'. This all happens within the same minute, at 11:24. A few moments pass and then you create Test Page C at 11:25. The 'Recent Changes' page looks like **Figure 8**.

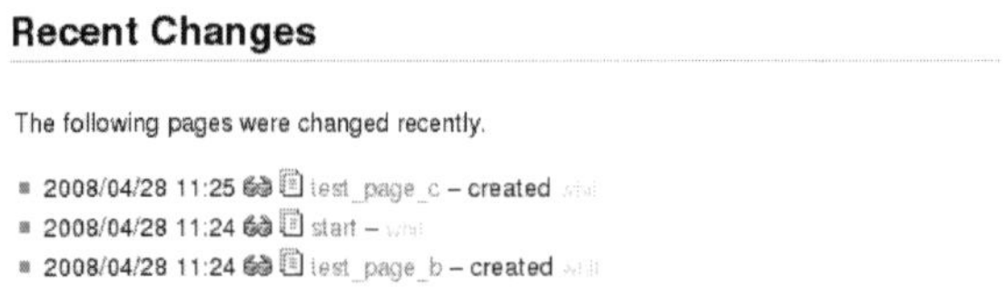

Recent Changes

The following pages were changed recently.

- 2008/04/28 11:25 🔗 📄 test_page_c – created ...
- 2008/04/28 11:24 🔗 📄 start – ...
- 2008/04/28 11:24 🔗 📄 test_page_b – created ...

Figure 8. *A list of recent changes made to pages in the wiki.*

This shows that you created 'Test Page B', then you edited 'start' (when you added the link to 'Test Page C'.) Then, a minute later, you created 'Test Page C'.

You're still not satisfied with the page, so a few minutes later, you go back and edit the 'start' page again, adding a link to 'Test Page D'. (But you don't get around to creating Test Page D yet.) The list of recent changes now shows the most recent edit to 'start' at 11:29, but not the previous edit at 11:24. See **Figure 9**.

Recent Changes

The following pages were changed recently.

- 2008/04/28 11:29 🔗 📄 start – ...
- 2008/04/28 11:25 🔗 📄 test_page_c – created ...
- 2008/04/28 11:24 🔗 📄 test_page_b – created ...

Figure 9. *Recent changes now shows only the most recent change to a page.*

In other words, you only get

```
11:29 edited start
11:25 edited C
11:24 edited B
```

not

```
11:29 edited start
11:25 edited C
11:24 edited start
11:24 edited B
```

You only see ***the most recent change*** to each page. (Use the 'View Old Revisions' function to see more detailed history on a single page.) Since a wiki is all about the content, this may not be sufficient for some folks, but that'd be a change you'd have to make to the DokuWiki code yourself.

Under the hood

Changes to the root folder are stored in /meta/_dokuwiki.changes. You can see all of the changes made to the entire namespace. Changes to an individual page are stored in the file /data/meta/<pagename>.changes. For example, start.changes contains the changes made to the start page. The _dokuwiki.changes page, then, is a combination of all of the other .changes files.

In a namespace, the <namespace>.changes file serves the same purpose as the _dokuwiki.changes page in the root.

Index of namespaces and pages

Clicking the "Sitemap" button in the lower right corner of a page will display a list of all namespaces and pages in the wiki. Namespaces (akin to folders) are listed first, in bold type, and then individual pages not contained within a namespace are listed below. Namespaces are collapsed by default (except for the current one). You can open a namespace by clicking on it. See **Figure 10**.

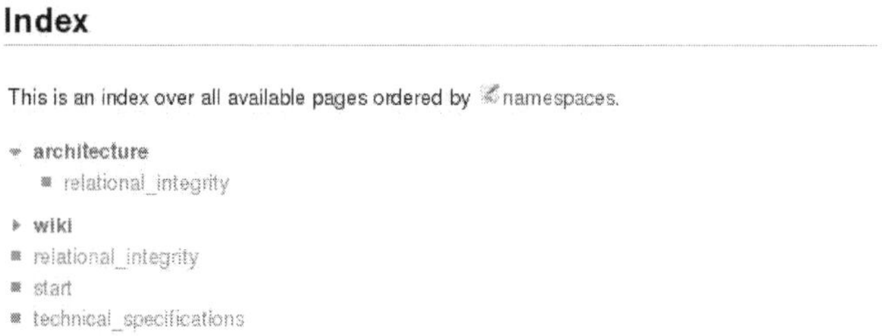

Index

This is an index over all available pages ordered by namespaces.

- ▾ **architecture**
  - ■ relational_integrity
- ▸ **wiki**
- ■ relational_integrity
- ■ start
- ■ technical_specifications

Figure 10. The Index shows namespaces and then individual pages.

Figure 10 shows the issue with naming a page with and without a namespace. The "Relational Integrity" page created in the root of the wiki is shown in the list as a green hyperlink (just like all other pages.) However, there's a second "Relational Integrity" hyperlink under the "architecture" namespace - this one was created using the "architecture:relational integrity" syntax instead of simply using the page name.

To return to the page you were on before clicking "Sitemap", click the "Show page" button.

Conclusion

In this chapter, we've discovered that DokuWiki is much more than software that enables editable Web pages. Indeed, it handles a large number of ancillary tasks, such as multi-user locking, caching for improved performance, and several version control features.

11: Your First Template

Templates are overlays to the basic DokuWiki appearance that allow you to customize its appearance.to your liking. Many templates also add configuration capabilities to extend the native functionality of DokuWiki. In this chapter, we'll install a template and examine the benefits it provides.

You might be asking "What's the difference between configuration and customization?" While intuitively you may know the difference, it's not so easy to define which is which, and, more importantly, where the line between them is. Generally, I think of configuration as settings to make the program operate properly while customization is settings to make the program work to your specification. Think of a car - you configure the car to have power steering and air conditioning. You customize the car with racing stripes and a custom paint job. What about dual exhausts? One could argue that they serve a functional purpose, but they're also often added merely for appearance sake.

What about a wiki-oriented example? In order to restrict access to the wiki, you would check the 'Use access control lists' checkbox in the Authentication Settings section of the Configuration Manager - yes, this is a configuration option. On the other hand, wanting to display a light purple as the background color or to remove the footers would be customization items. There are some grey areas - would the display of a table of contents of a page be functional or strictly for appearance? Difficult to say, and I would suppose that there are folks who could argue successfully on both sides of the issue.

Enough semantics. Templates do both.

Template basics

The default appearance of DokuWiki (colors, position of buttons, fonts) can be changed via the use of templates. Some software applications call this 'skinning' - applying different skins to change the appearance of the application. Media players were one of the first to do so - many moons ago, I spent hours with XMMS downloading and trying out different skins. Other software applications such as word processors and Web pages call them styles.

Choosing a template

Template interact with the core DokuWiki software. As a result, as DokuWiki gets upgraded, templates often need to be upgraded in concert. However, the template designer doesn't always do so, and thus templates can become deprecated. Fortunately, you don't have to guess which templates are current.

In the Basic Settings section of the Configuration Manager, the fourth setting is "Template" and out of the box, this control is disabled because DokuWiki only comes with one template ('default'). You can download additional templates from the dokuwiki.org site at /Templates - there are nearly 150 templates to choose from. And you could create your own if you were so inclined.

`http://www.dokuwiki.org/Templates`

This list of template is grouped by version of DokuWiki; the most recent version first. Not only does this help you select current templates but also allows you to find templates that work with earlier versions of DokuWiki as well.

The nifty thing about DokuWiki templates, unlike those Media Player skins, is that they're not strictly appearance oriented. Many templates also provide additional functionality, so they address configuration and customization at the same time. Let's take a look at one template that does both: Adora Dark Template.

The 'Adora Dark Template' template traces its heritage from the Adora Belle style from 2012, which has been the default DokuWiki template since inception.

A navigation box and a toolbox on the left, the ability to add your own logo to the upper left corner, and a tab-based interface for editing pages and viewing old revisions are all features of Adora Dark. I love it. Let's install and use it.

Installing a template

Installing a template for the most recent versions of DokuWiki can be done from within DokuWiki; earlier versions require you to download the template archive and put it into the lib/tpl folder.

To install a template, click the Admin link (obviously, you have to be an admin user) and select the Extension Manager. Click on the Search and Install tab, and search for "Adora" in the Search Extension text box. See **Figure 1**.

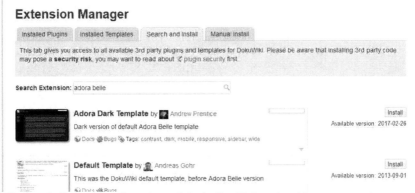

Figure 1. *Searching for a template in the Extension Manager.*

Note that the version date is under the Install button on the right side.

Even better, you can get additional information on the template by clicking the down arrow in the center of page, as shown in **Figure 2**.

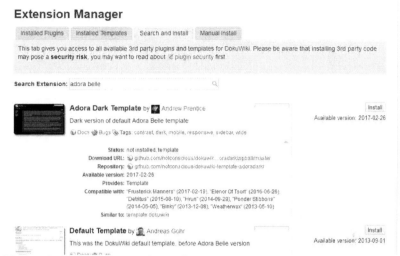

Figure 2. *Additional template information.*

Click on the Install button on the right side and after a moment, if it goes well, you'll see a message as shown in **Figure 3**.

You are here: start
Trace: - start

Template adoradark installed successfully

Extension Manager

| Installed Plugins | Installed Templates | Search and Install | Manual Install |

This tab gives you access to all available 3rd party plugins and templates for DokuWil may pose a **security risk**, you may want to read about plugin security first.

Search Extension:

Figure 3. *A successful template install.*

Under the hood, a new folder has been created under lib\tpl, adoradark. Inside the folder, you'll see a complete folder structure as shown in **Figure 4**.

Name ▲	Ext	Size
css		
images		
lang		
lib		
.gitignore		11
adoradark.jpg	jpg	870,032
CHANGELOG.md	md	542
detail.php	php	5,029
main.php	php	4,849
manager.dat	dat	129
mediamanager.php	php	1,397
README.md	md	1,193
script.js	js	2,343
style.ini	ini	3,310
template.info.txt	txt	211
tpl_footer.php	php	1,667
tpl_header.php	php	3,257

Figure 4. *Files installed with a new template.*

Now that the template has been installed, you can see it, along with all other installed templates, in the Installed Templates tab of the Extension Manager, as shown in **Figure 5**.

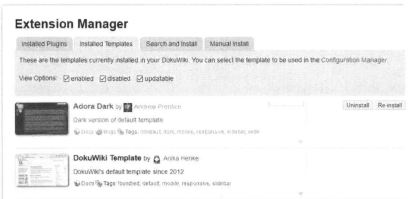

Figure 5. *All installed templates.*

You'll notice the Uninstall and Reinstall buttons on the right side for all templates except the default DokuWiki Template.

Now that the template has been installed, that template will automagically appear as a choice in the Template combo box in the Configuration Manager, as shown in **Figure 6**.

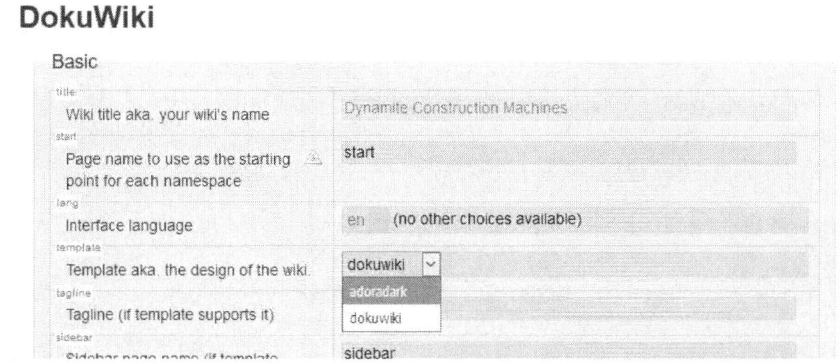

DokuWiki

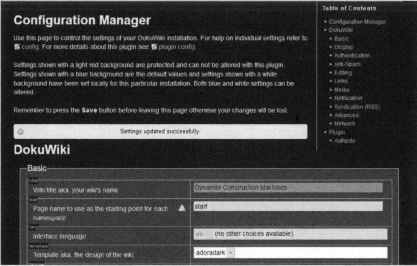

Figure 6. *The template combo is now populated with the new template.*

After choosing a new template, you'll have to click the Save button at the very bottom of the Configuration Manager; doing so applies the new Adora Dark template, as shown in **Figure 7**.

Figure 7. *The Adora Dark template applied.*

Some templates have additional configuration steps; those are described in the instructions that come with that template, which you can find in the Docs link on the Installed Template page of the Extension Manager. We always read the docs first. I mean, last.

As you can see, things look a lot different all of a sudden - just from installing a template!

New settings

One of the magical things about the DokuWiki architecture and the associated templates is that selecting a template may automatically modify the settings displayed in the Configuration Manager. While the Adora Dark template doesn't, others do. For example, the Dokubook template adds three new settings to the Configuration manager, as shown in **Figure 8**.

Template Settings

Dokubook Template Settings

tpl»dokubook»sb_pagename		
Pagename to use for the navigation		navigation
tpl»dokubook»ft_pagename		
Pagename to use for the footer		footer
tpl»dokubook»closedwiki		
Closed Wiki (Navigation shows only the login form if not logged in)		☐

Figure 8. New settings added as a result of selecting the Dokubook template.

Pretty nifty, eh?

Let's talk about these settings, because they're all pretty useful.

Pagename to use for the navigation/footer

The first two settings determine the name of the file used to display the contents of the navigation box and the custom footer on the page. The defaults are 'navigation' and 'footer'. If the 'navigation' file doesn't exist, the Dokubook template will automatically generate the contents and display those Namespaces and Pagenames. If the 'footer.txt' file doesn't exist, no footer will be displayed.

I've covered how to work with a sidebar in Chapter 6. Let's discuss how to add a footer.

Adding a footer

Working with a footer is similar. Create a text file named 'footer.txt' and put it in the root of the data/pages folder. Like navigation, the optimal method is to temporarily create a link named 'footer' on your home/start page, edit and add contents, and save it. Once the footer displays on the page, you'll see an 'Edit' button in the footer as well. Finally, remove the temporarily link to 'footer' from your home page.

A file with the following contents

```
This is a sample custom file.
```

results in the page shown in **Figure 9**.

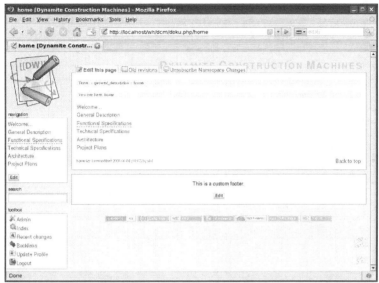

Figure 9. *A custom footer, courtesy of the Dokubook template.*

Notice the "Edit" button at the bottom of the footer block; use it to modify the text of 'footer.txt' once you've created it. If you decide later that you don't want a footer, you can either click Edit, remove all of the text, and then Save, which automatically deletes the page (just like deleting any other page), or you can manually go into the file system and delete 'footer.txt' in the data/pages folder of your DokuWiki installation.

Closed Wiki (Navigation shows only...)

When you navigate to a wiki with the Dokubook template applied, and that page requires login, curious things happen. The navigation and toolbox boxes are visible and fully populated, again, even before you login. Also, even though DokuWiki knows you haven't logged in yet, it asks you "Perhaps you forgot to login?" anyway. See **Figure 10**.

Hentzenwerke Publishing, Inc.
books@hentzenwerke.com • www.hentzenwerke.com

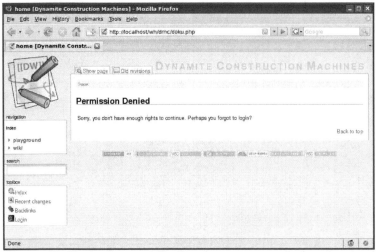

Figure 10. *Navigation and Toolbox boxes appear before logging in.*

Part of the point of requiring a login is to hide the content of the wiki from the casual visitor who just happens by. So the contents of the navigation page and the boxes are a problem. The request about logging in, that's not a big deal; it just annoys me. The first problem can be solved by checking the "Closed Wiki" checkbox setting. Doing so changes the initial page to that shown in **Figure 11**.

Figure 11. *Selecting the 'Closed Wiki' setting hides the navigation and toolbox boxes.*

If you take a look in the conf/local.php file now, you'll see a new setting:

```
$conf['tpl']['dokubook']['closedwiki'] = 1;
```

Hentzenwerke Publishing, Inc.
books@hentzenwerke.com • www.hentzenwerke.com

One solution to the "Permission denied" question is to alter the contents of the index.php file in the wiki root. The original contents contains the following line:

```
header("Location: doku.php");
```

This line inserts the 'doku.php' command into the URL. What you want is more information in the form of additional parameters, like so:

```
header("Location: doku.php?id=home&do=login");
```

Change the line in the index.php file to this and you'll be all set. The login page will be loaded instead of 'home.txt'. See **Figure 12**.

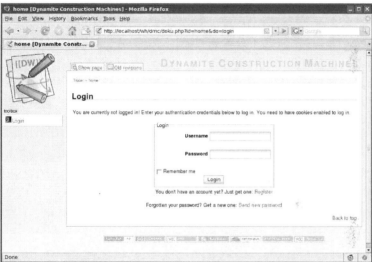

Figure 12. Modifying index.php to force the login page to appear.

Conclusion

Templates allow you to customize the appearance, and often add functionality, to your Dokuwiki installation. With over 50 templates available, there's bound to be one that suits your needs.

12: Your First Plugins

A plugin is a piece of software that adds functionality to a DokuWiki installation without having to modify the DokuWiki source code itself. There are hundreds (yes, hundreds) of plugins that do everything from displaying image galleries to formatting a molecular formula to generating an easy to use to-do list following the principles of David Allen's GTD time management system. In this chapter, we'll get started with plugins by installing a favorite plugin or three of mine.

True to its open source roots, DokuWiki's architecture supports the ability for third parties to extend the basic DokuWiki functionality, and the DokuWiki community has whole-heartedly taken it up on its offer; to date, there are more than 1200 plugins available. The list of these plugins is found at

`http://www.dokuwiki.org/plugins`

and can be somewhat overwhelming. No one wants to read through hundreds of descriptions to find the one that they're looking for to fill some specific need. On the left side of the page, the list is divided by type, but even this produces a long list. Fortunately, DokuWiki's plugin page has a second search mechanism called a tag cloud to categorize and index each plugin, making it easy to find potential matches based on one or more keywords. If you're not familiar with a tag cloud, let's take a look at DokuWiki's use of one.

The tag cloud world of DokuWiki plugins

A tag cloud is a collection of user-generated keywords that are visually organized to represent the content and frequency of individual elements in a collection of items. First conceived for use with weblogs, tag clouds have evolved to be used in additional contexts, such as the DokuWiki list of plugins.

Each plugin is assigned (by the author, and perhaps others as well) one or more keywords that describe the plugin. The keywords for all of the plugins are merged into one list and displayed in a single 'blob' of words - the result appears much like a cloud. The frequency of appearance in the list drives how big a specific keyword is displayed; popular keywords like 'email' or 'image', used in many plugins, would be larger than very specific keywords, like 'gravity' or 'Egyptian', that are used in only a couple of plugins. The DokuWiki tag cloud is shown in **Figure 1**.

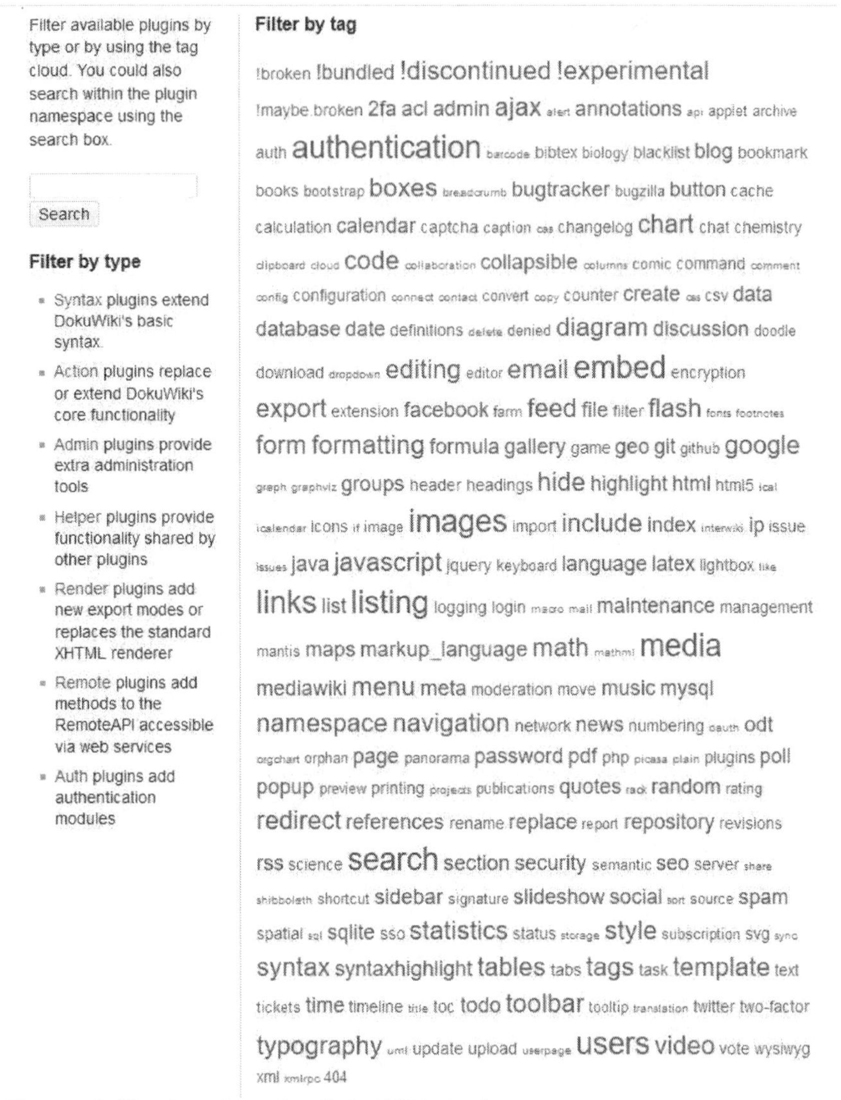

Filter available plugins by type or by using the tag cloud. You could also search within the plugin namespace using the search box.

Search

Filter by type

- Syntax plugins extend DokuWiki's basic syntax.
- Action plugins replace or extend DokuWiki's core functionality
- Admin plugins provide extra administration tools
- Helper plugins provide functionality shared by other plugins
- Render plugins add new export modes or replaces the standard XHTML renderer
- Remote plugins add methods to the RemoteAPI accessible via web services
- Auth plugins add authentication modules

Filter by tag

!broken !bundled !discontinued !experimental !maybe broken 2fa acl admin ajax alert annotations api applet archive auth authentication barcode bibtex biology blacklist blog bookmark books bootstrap boxes breadcrumb bugtracker bugzilla button cache calculation calendar captcha caption css changelog chart chat chemistry clipboard cloud code collaboration collapsible columns comic command comment config configuration connect contact convert copy counter create css csv data database date definitions delete denied diagram discussion doodle download dropdown editing editor email embed encryption export extension facebook farm feed file filter flash fonts footnotes form formatting formula gallery game geo git github google graph graphviz groups header headings hide highlight html html5 ical icalendar icons if image images import include index interwiki ip issue issues java javascript jquery keyboard language latex lightbox like links list listing logging login macro mail maintenance management mantis maps markup_language math mathml media mediawiki menu meta moderation move music mysql namespace navigation network news numbering oauth odt orgchart orphan page panorama password pdf php picasa plain plugins poll popup preview printing projects publications quotes rack random rating redirect references rename replace report repository revisions rss science search section security semantic seo server share shibboleth shortcut sidebar signature slideshow social sort source spam spatial sql sqlite sso statistics status storage style subscription svg sync syntax syntaxhighlight tables tabs tags task template text tickets time timeline title toc todo toolbar tooltip translation twitter two-factor typography uml update upload userpage users video vote wysiwyg xml xmlrpc 404

Figure 1. *The tag cloud for DokuWiki plugins.*

Searching for a plugin that meets a specific need, then is simply a matter of searching for one or more words that describe that need (such as 'graph' or 'pdf') and clicking on it in the cloud. For example, clicking on 'email' in the tag cloud result in a list of plugins that have the 'email' keyword in the description. See **Figure 2**.

Tagged with 'email' (20)			
			Show all (remove filter/sort)
Plugin	**Author**	**Last Update**	**Popularity**
Compatible with DokuWiki? **2017-02-19 "Frusterick Manners"**			
Bureaucracy Plugin ⬇ Download		2017-07-27	▭
Easily create HTML forms to collect data which can be sent via email or used to create pages.			
Provides: Syntax, Action **Tags:** create, email, form, poll ✉ Andreas Gohr			
SMTP Plugin ⬇ Download		2017-08-03	▭
Configure a SMTP server (with optional auth) for sending mails from within DokuWiki			
Provides: Admin, Action **Tags:** email, smtp, smtpauth ✉ Andreas Gohr			
Two Factor Authentication - SMS Gateway Plugin ⬇ Download		2017-08-05	▭
SMS email gateway support plugin for the Two Factor Authentication			

Figure 2.Results of a tag cloud search for 'email'.

Figure 2 is just a partial list – there were 20 matches in the full list. Referring back to Figure 2, look at the list of plugins. Two columns in particular deserve mention. The second from the right, Last Update, can be used for a quick check to see how recent the plugin is, and thus how likely the plugin will work with the most recent version of DokuWiki. (If the Last Update date is shortly after the release of a version, that's a pretty good indication that the plugin has been updated for that version.) The far right column, popularity, shows a horizontal bar that for most plugins will be empty for a while. The data that populates this bar comes from an plugin that was introduced in the 2008/05/05 version. It doesn't seem to be collecting much data.

Installing plugins

There are two methods to install a plugin. The first is to use the plugin manager on the Admin page (the plugin manager itself is a plugin, albeit one that's included with the base DokuWiki installation, in a curious case of self-referential architecture.) The second method is a manual install, where you download the files, unzip them, and move them into your DokuWiki site. Some plugins don't install reliably - or at all - with the plugin manager, so we'll walk through examples of both mechanisms.

The Extension Manager

Access the plugin manager via the Extension Manager on the Admin page. **Figure 3** shows the Installed Plugins Manager with some default plugins and a few optional plugins installed.

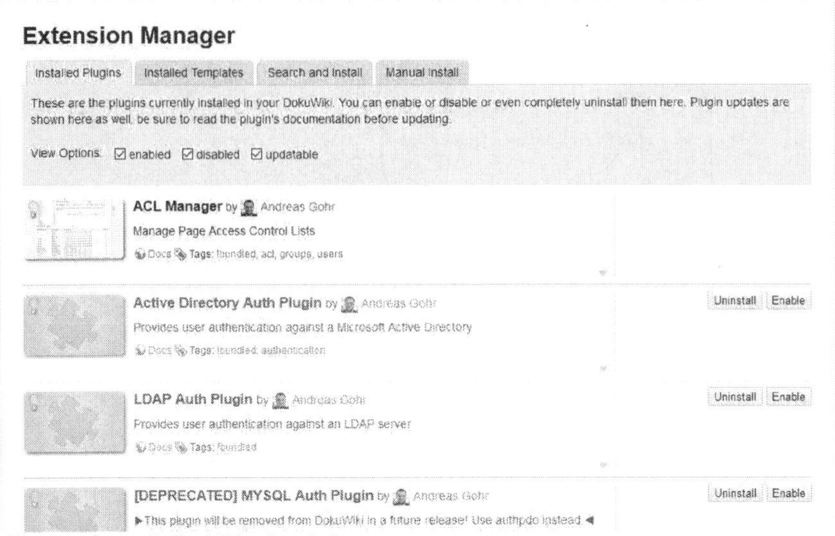

Extension Manager

| Installed Plugins | Installed Templates | Search and Install | Manual Install |

These are the plugins currently installed in your DokuWiki. You can enable or disable or even completely uninstall them here. Plugin updates are shown here as well, be sure to read the plugin's documentation before updating.

View Options: ☑ enabled ☑ disabled ☑ updatable

ACL Manager by Andreas Gohr
Manage Page Access Control Lists
Docs Tags: bundled, acl, groups, users

Active Directory Auth Plugin by Andreas Gohr   Uninstall Enable
Provides user authentication against a Microsoft Active Directory
Docs Tags: bundled, authentication

LDAP Auth Plugin by Andreas Gohr   Uninstall Enable
Provides user authentication against an LDAP server
Docs Tags: bundled

[DEPRECATED] MYSQL Auth Plugin by Andreas Gohr   Uninstall Enable
▶ This plugin will be removed from DokuWiki in a future release! Use authpdo instead ◀

Figure 3. Installed Plugins tab.

To use the Extension Manager to install a plugin, find the plugin of interest, either via the tagcloud or by clicking on the Search tab, similar to searching for a template in Chapter 11. For example, searching on 'statistics' results in a list like that shown in **Figure 4**.

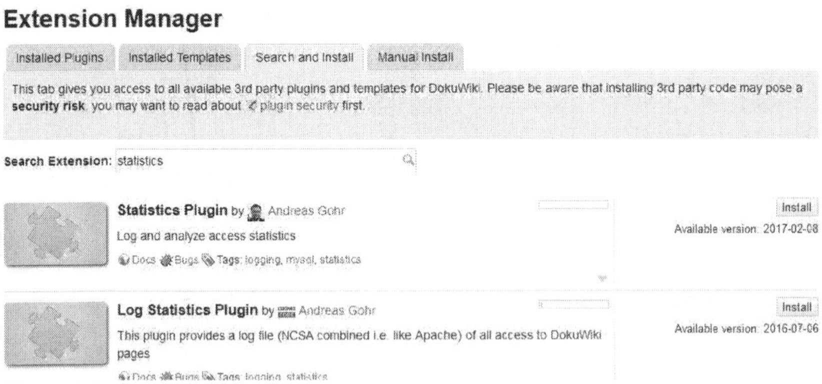

Extension Manager

| Installed Plugins | Installed Templates | Search and Install | Manual Install |

This tab gives you access to all available 3rd party plugins and templates for DokuWiki. Please be aware that installing 3rd party code may pose a **security risk**, you may want to read about plugin security first.

Search Extension: statistics

Statistics Plugin by Andreas Gohr   Install
Log and analyze access statistics   Available version: 2017-02-08
Docs Bugs Tags: logging, mysql, statistics

Log Statistics Plugin by Andreas Gohr   Install
This plugin provides a log file (NCSA combined i.e. like Apache) of all access to DokuWiki   Available version: 2016-07-06
pages
Docs Bugs Tags: logging, statistics

Figure 4. Statistics plugins.

Installing works the same way as with templates; clicking on the Install button on the right downloads and installs the plugin, this time in a new folder in the lib\plugins folder.

Once installed, an additional section in the Configuration Manager will likely be added. See the bottom of the Table of Contents in the upper left of **Figure 5**.

Configuration Manager

Use this page to control the settings of your DokuWiki installation. For help on individual settings refer to ☑ config. For more details about this plugin see ☑ plugin.config.

Settings shown with a light red background are protected and can not be altered with this plugin. Settings shown with a blue background are the default values and settings shown with a white background have been set locally for this particular installation. Both blue and white settings can be altered.

Remember to press the **Save** button before leaving this page otherwise your changes will be lost.

DokuWiki

Basic

title Wiki title aka. your wiki's name		Dynamite Construction Machines
start Page name to use as the starting point for each namespace	⚠	start
lang Interface language		en (no other choices available)

Figure 5. The link to the new QuickStats section in the Configuration Manager appears at the bottom of the Table of Contents.

Clicking on the link navigates to the section of settings, as shown in **Figure 6**.

Quickstats

plugin»quickstats»excludes Comma separated list of ip addresses that should not be counted in statistics	!!not set!!
plugin»quickstats»aborts Comma separated list of nuisance ip addresses that should not be given access to the site	!!not set!!
plugin»quickstats»geoip_local Maxmind GeoLiteCity.dat will be found in the quickstats dir: quickstats/GEOIP	☐
plugin»quickstats»geoip_dir Maxmind GeoLiteCity.dat directory; quickstats will look here if geoip_local (i.e. quickstats/GEOIP) is not selected	/usr/local/share/GeoIP/
plugin»quickstats»geoplugin Use the web-based geoPlugin for IP geo-locating (defaults to true); with this set to true GeoLiteCity.dat is not needed	☑
plugin»quickstats»long_names Maximum number of characters when displaying long names. set to	25

Figure 6. The QuickStats section in the Configuration Manager.

Manual install

Plugins are located their own folders in lib/plugins/. For example, the 'gallery' plugin is located in lib/plugins/gallery folder, the 'box' plugin is located in the lib/plugins/boxes folder. The manual installation process generally involves downloading, unzipping and copying the plugin files to a folder in lib/plugins. This process is described in detail with an actual example using the Gallery plugin in a subsequent section.

The Box plugin

Perhaps the most glaring failing of a wiki is that users are increasingly used to exotic looking Web pages, complete with JavaScript and AJAX interactive functionality, Flash media, and carefully crafted layouts involving complex images and designs. Next to these million dollar road shows, a simple Wiki page with pages and pages of plain text seems downright old-fashioned.

The 'box' plugin allows a user to add some pizazz to their pages, highlighting pieces of the page with rounded and colored boxes, using simple syntax tags similar to those you've used like <code>.

Installing the Boxes plugin manually

Download the plugin, unzip, create a folder named 'boxes', and copy the files into the lib\plugins\boxes folder. However, when you look at the installed plugin list, you'll see a warning that 'boxes' is the wrong folder name, as shown in **Figure 7**.

Figure 7. Plugin installation warning.

Using the Boxes plugin

The basic syntax for a box is surrounding the text you want boxed with <box> and </box> tags:

```
<box>This text will be in a box.</box>
```

See **Figure 8** for an example.

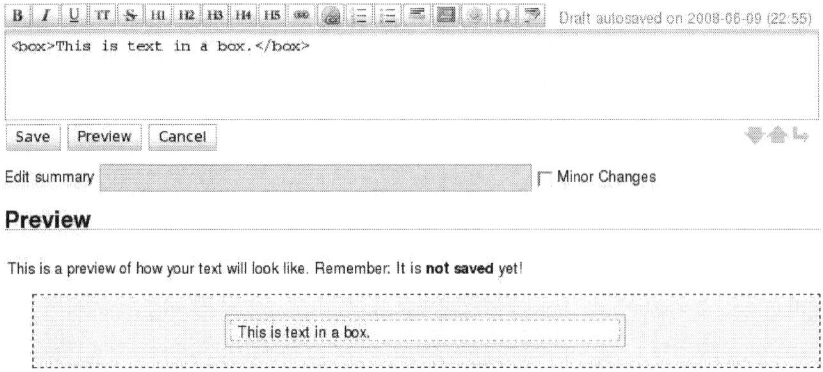

Figure 8. The code to create a box and it's result.

There are a number of extensions to the basic syntax. Both tags can contain text that will be displayed on the top and bottom of the box, respectively:

```
<box|this text is a title>This is text in a box</box|this text is a
caption>
```

The leading tag can also contain strings controlling the width of the box (e.g. 80%) and the appearance of the box (e.g. colors):

```
<box 80%|this text is a title>This is text in a box</box|this text is a
caption>
<box left orange>This is text in a box</box>
```

See **Figure 9** for the results.

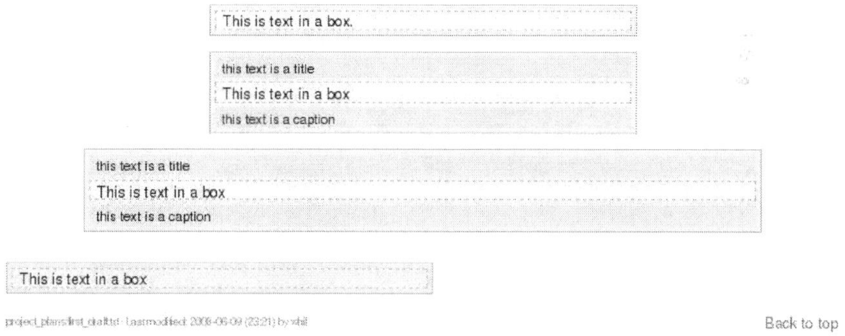

Figure 9. *Multiple examples of boxes using the 'boxes' plugin.*

Boxes can be nested (contained in other boxes) and a wide variety of other DokuWiki formatted texts can be embedded in a box.

The Cloud plugin

Another simple but useful example of a plugin demonstrates the "cloud" functionality that was used to find plugins earlier in this chapter.

First, search for the 'cloud' plugin and install it.

Second, create a new page in your wiki, titled, perhaps, 'cloud'. Then add the following text to the page:

```
~~CLOUD~~
```

Upon saving the page, the tag cloud will be displayed as shown in **Figure 10**.

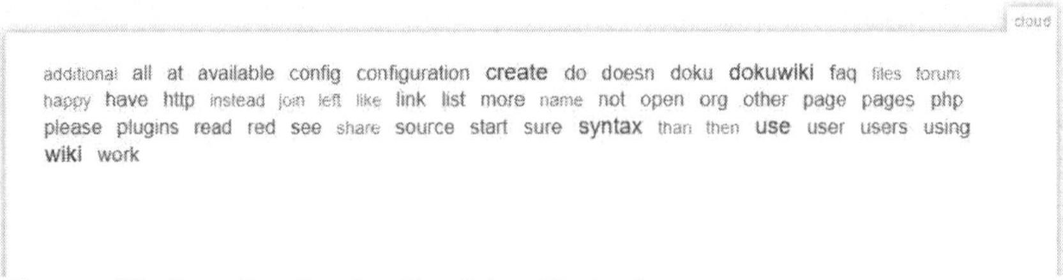

additional all at available config configuration create do doesn doku dokuwiki faq files forum happy have http instead join left like link list more name not open org other page pages php please plugins read red see share source start sure syntax than then use user users using wiki work

Figure 10. Results of using the "cloud" plugin.

You may have to hit the Refresh button in your browser to get the tags to display in proper proportion.

Plugin Philosophies

Now that I've piqued your interest in extending DokuWiki via plugins, it's time to bring you back down to Earth with a couple of cautions regarding security and upgradability. Then I'll finish up by considering a strategy for deploying plugins with some consistency.

Security concerns

First, about security. Plugins are programs written by third parties; neither the programs nor the third parties have undergone any type of vetting. This means that Bad Things could happen to your system when a plugin is installed - either through the malicious intent of an author bent on using DokuWiki for evil rather than good, or (more likely), through a goofy programming error errantly exposing a vulnerability.

Fortunately, there are things you can do to mitigate potential harm. First, see how popular the plugin is, how much effort has been put into building and maintaining it, and the general support it has. A plugin that was released four years ago, has never been upgraded, and has no comments or questions may be on shakier ground than a plugin that is often recommended on the forums and lists, has been regularly updated for new versions, and has lots of release notes.

Second, if you don't know, ask around on the forums and lists. There are lots of plugins that do not see as much attention simply because they address an obscure need. Image and email plugins are more popular than those that deal with formatting ancient language scripts.

Third, if you have the chops, look at the source code. This is open source, after all, You're allowed to look - heck, you're encouraged to look!

Upgradability ramifications

Suppose your wiki depends on a certain plugin to deliver critical functionality. Then DokuWiki is upgraded. What if your plugin isn't upgraded to work with the new version? Either you're stuck with an old version or you lose that critical functionality. Neither is an optimal situation to find yourself in.

Additionally, for DokuWiki installed in other languages, the translation may not be up to date: some words may not be translated.

Similar to the ideas for dealing with security, you have some options here. Popular plugins with a lot of support are more likely to be upgraded than a one-off plugin that some one wrote once for a specific need, and hasn't touched since. You also have the opportunity, since it's open source, to take the plugin and update it yourself - given that you have the ability, or can find someone who does.

Note that I bring this up more as a cautionary tale than to scare you away. Most plugins should continue to work, because the syntax plugin API is very stable. There are a few plugins that are nearly as old as DokuWiki itself and still work. The admin and action plugin APIs were more in flux in the early days but are now pretty stable as well. So it will generally be more the exception than the rule to find a plugin that no longer performs.

Deploying plugins with consistency

The examples in this chapter have all installed a plugin directly into a specific wiki. As you use plugins, you will likely find a number that you use over and over, and it can all of a sudden get confusing trying to remember which plugins are installed in which wikis. It can then get even worse when creating a new wiki - you have to go and grab copies of each plugin you want, and more often than not, you'll forget the one that you most need for this new installation.

For this reason, I use a master DokuWiki installation in which I install all my plugins. Then, when I roll out a new wiki, all of my plugins come along for the ride.

Conclusion

In this chapter, I've introduced the use of plugins as a way to extend the core DokuWiki functionality, and taken a look at how two popular plugins work. I've also mentioned two areas of concern that you should be aware of; not to kill your interest in plugins, but simply to make you aware that the use of plugins is a responsibility as well as a privilege.

13: Deploying and Upgrading

Because DokuWiki is just files, deployment from development to production is a simple process, to the point of being trivial. Upgrading isn't much harder. As a result, you're probably going to finish this chapter before you're done with your next chocolate chip cookie, and your glass of milk will certainly still be cold.

Simple to the point of trivial doesn't mean not worth mentioning, though. Pushing the power button or clicking the start button to access a menu may seem trivial once you've done it - but the process is critically important to know how to do until then. And there are a couple of tips that might make the process easier.

Deploying DokuWiki to a production site

I'm assuming you've got a development machine to do your testing and experimenting with, and will then deploy to a production box when you're happy with your wiki.

General concept

The basic idea is to install on a development machine, configuring and setting up users and access permissions, and creating as much content as you can to start, and then copying the whole folder structure to a production machine. This is a lot easier, safer, and more reliable than trying to do a full install on a production machine.

Your production machine may take one of several forms - it could be a different box on your LAN (or WAN), or on a separate network altogether. Or maybe you're deploying to an ISP's box - either in the form of a dedicated host, a VPS, or a shared host.

When it all comes down to it, these targets can be separated into two categories - those where you have complete access to the box, and those where you've got limited access, access to just your own Web root.

In all cases, you'll need to be able to copy or FTP files from your development box to the production machine (if you can't do at least this, it's time to find a different production machine). The only difference is dealing with permissions; a shared host may have more restrictive permissions and your access/ability to change them may be limited. The worst case is that you have to get the administrator of the box to tweak them during the initial copying. The DokuWiki forum and mailing list are both chock full of suggestions about working around various problems.

Specific issues

The biggest issue you'll have to deal with is deciding where on your production server you want to put your wiki. The choice you make depends on whether your wiki will be the entire site (www.example.com goes straight to your wiki's home page) or if your wiki will be part of a larger site (www.example.com has a link for "statistics wiki" which goes to your wiki's home page.) Let's address both.

When the wiki is your entire site

The first is fairly straight forward. On your Web host, you'll have a Web root folder. In Red Hat distributions of Linux, this is /var/www/html by default, in Windows, this is c:\inetpub\wwwroot. The main DokuWiki files go here, like so:

```
doku.php
feed.php
index.php
```

and the rest of the DokuWiki folder structure goes underneath. In Linux, then, you'd see:

```
/var/www/html/doku.php
/var/www/html/feed.php
/var/www/html/index.php
/var/www/html/bin
/var/www/html/conf
/var/www/html/data
/var/www/html/inc
/var/www/html/lib
```

And in Windows, you'd see:

```
\inetpub\wwwroot\doku.php
\inetpub\wwwroot\feed.php
\inetpub\wwwroot\index.php
\inetpub\wwwroot\bin
\inetpub\wwwroot\conf
\inetpub\wwwroot\data
\inetpub\wwwroot\inc
\inetpub\wwwroot\lib
```

As we discussed in Chapter 3, you do NOT want to keep install.php on your production server. If you've configured your Web host to see 'index.php' as a default document, then your work is basically done; navigating to the URL mapped to the Web root will automatically run index.php which then runs doku.php.

Making your wiki part of a larger site

When your wiki is just one piece of a Web site, then the production server folder structure differs a bit. Suppose your Web site has a folder structure like so:

```
/var/www/html/index.main
/var/www/html/index.css
/var/www/html/admin
```

```
/var/www/html/images
/var/www/html/labs
/var/www/html/manufacturing
/var/www/html/sales
/var/www/html/web
/var/www/html/xander
/var/www/html/zen
```

and links on your home page included the following

```
Admin   Labs   Manufacturing   Sales   Web   Xander   Zen
```

Now you want to add a wiki to handle statistics to your site. For simplicity's sake, we'll just add a "Stats" link like so:

```
Admin   Labs   Manufacturing   Sales   Stats   Web   Xander   Zen
```

and add a folder under the main Web root:

```
/var/www/html/statswiki
```

Your entire DokuWiki folder structure goes into this 'wiki' folder, like so:

```
/var/www/html/statswiki/doku.php
/var/www/html/statswiki/feed.php
/var/www/html/statswiki/index.php
/var/www/html/statswiki/bin
/var/www/html/statswiki/conf
/var/www/html/statswiki/data
/var/www/html/statswiki/inc
/var/www/html/statswiki/lib
```

And the link for "Stats" on the main page points to "statswiki/index.php". Since everything inside DokuWiki is relatively addressed, you're done!

Shared host example

Deployment on a shared host is easy **past** the point of being trivial. With my host, all I had to do was create a "cust_one" folder underneath my main website and then FTP the entire DokuWiki folder structure there. Then, users just had to navigate to www.whilhentzen.com/cust_one. Since the index.php was defined as a default document, it was automatically executed when they navigated to the folder, and they were immediately presented with the login page for their own wiki.

Down on the Farm

If you're going to be doing multiple installs of DokuWiki, you may be thinking that it's a nuisance to perform the same steps over and over again, and it well may be. If you're adventurous, you can try what's known as a "farm install" where a single installation of the DokuWiki source code will support multiple sites.

In a farm install, one copy of the source code - called the 'farmer' - is configured to run several child instances - called 'animals'. There are two advantages to such a setup, and one disadvantage. The advantages are that only a single installation is needed, and, correspondingly, only this engine needs to be upgraded. The disadvantage is that the configuration is complex and requires a good deal of manual modification and advanced knowledge.

Depending on your philosophy, you should also understand that plugins and templates are installed in the farmer, so they are common to all animals (but plugins can be enabled/disabled in each animal.)

There's a wiki page at www.dokuwiki.org that describes how to use a farm install:

```
http://www.dokuwiki.org/tips:farm
```

Upgrading DokuWiki to a new version
You've now got a live wiki and a copy of it on your development box. Your users have gone mad with delight... they're using it every day, creating pages with wild abandon. And then a new version of DokuWiki comes along.

How do you know when a new version is available?
If the "Check for updates and security warnings?" setting in the "Advanced Settings" section of the Configuration Manager is checked (as it is by default), a message indicating a new version (or a security update) is available will display at the top of every page. This message is visible only to superusers if ACL is enabled (after the user has logged in), or to all users otherwise. See Figure 17 of Chapter 8.

The big picture
Since a DokuWiki wiki simply consists of text files, with configuration and data clearly separated from code, an upgrade is basically a matter of copying files. The "install:upgrade" topic on the DokuWiki wiki provides the easy way - unpack, check the changelog, and then, after you back up your production site, copy the new files over the old ones of your installation. Yes, that's it - no 'update' programs that fiddle with EXEs, mess with databases, or install new and delete old widgets behind the scenes. Just moving text files to and fro.

However, the process can be a bit more involved than that, in that you may be working with templates and plugins that you need to test with the new version of DokuWiki. But it's still pretty simple - copying your site from the production server to the development area, doing an upgrade, testing the upgraded site, and copying the new files back.

Hentzenwerke Publishing, Inc.
books@hentzenwerke.com • www.hentzenwerke.com

Things not to do

When I was starting out with DokuWiki, I would test an upgrade by creating a new installation, with the new version, on my development box. Then I'd install the templates and plugins that I was using, and test them out. Next, I'd copy my live configuration and data from the production site to the new site on the development box, and test again. Finally, once satisfied that everything was running fine, I'd copy the entire site from my development box back to the production box.

However, while this process provided much piece of mind, and allowed me to practice manipulating the DokuWiki infrastructure, it also messed up the modification times of all the files that came from the production site - and so when the new version was deployed, it looked like every page had been changed. Good idea for dinking around. Bad idea for real use.

So let's look at the right way to do it, in detail.

Step by step upgrade process

Again, before we begin, back up your production wiki.

Create an installation with the new DokuWiki version

The first step is to create an installation with the new version of DokuWiki on your development machine. I typically do this alongside the current installation, renaming the current first, and then creating the new installation with the current installation's old folder name.

For example, suppose I have a wiki called 'stats' for my Dynamite Construction Machines customer. In my Sites folder on my development machine, I'd have the following structure:

```
/Sites/wh/dcm/stats
```

This contains a backup copy of the production wiki. The full structure looks like this:

```
/Sites/wh/dcm/stats
/Sites/wh/dcm/stats/doku.php
/Sites/wh/dcm/stats/feed.php
/Sites/wh/dcm/stats/index.php
/Sites/wh/dcm/stats/bin
/Sites/wh/dcm/stats/conf
/Sites/wh/dcm/stats/data
/Sites/wh/dcm/stats/inc
/Sites/wh/dcm/stats/lib
/Sites/wh/dcm/stats/vendor
```

While a reputable hosting company would have a reliable backup strategy, I'm a belt and suspenders kind of guy, so I regularly archive off the data folder from the server to the data folder on my local machine, like so:

```
/Sites/wh/dcm/stats/data_201701
```

```
/Sites/wh/dcm/stats/data_201702
/Sites/wh/dcm/stats/data_201703
```

Supposing I was doing the upgrade on June 1, I'd rename that folder (on my local machine) to stats_20170601. Then I'd create a new installation on my local machine with the brand new version of DokuWiki, naming that new folder 'stats'. (This new installation could come straight from the unzipped version of DokuWiki as described in Chapter 3.) When I was done with all the renaming and new installations and whatnot, I'd have:

```
/Sites/wh/dcm/stats          (contains a new, empty wiki w/ latest DS)
/Sites/wh/dcm/stats_20170601 (contains the backup from the server)
```

Install and test templates
The second step is to install - into the new, empty wiki you just created - all templates that your production installation uses, and then test them. This step has several parts. First, identify the templates you've got installed in your production version and add those to your new installation. Next, look for updates to those templates, and install them as you find them. Finally, run through your wiki, making sure the key features and functions of each template work as expected. This shouldn't be too big a chore, as most templates can be expected to work right out of the box with future versions of DokuWiki.

Install and test plugins
The third step is to install all plugins - also into the new, empty wiki that you juste created - that your current installation uses, and then test them as well. Depending on how many templates and plugins you have, you might choose to do this in parallel with the template step.

As you'll read in Chapter 15, I use a master installation source folder that already has the templates and plugins that I regularly use installed, so, if you've followed that technique, your new installation will likely have at least some of those templates and plugins. However, it's possible that you've also added third party add-ins for this specific wiki installation. Here's where you add them in and make sure they run on an empty wiki.

These two steps can be challenging in that it's possible that not all templates and plugins that you're using with the previous version have been upgraded to work with the latest DokuWiki version.

You don't want to just take your current versions and plug them into your new DokuWiki installation; better to look at the templates and plugins pages on the DokuWiki wiki to see if they've been updated to work with the new version of DokuWiki. There could be subtle (and undesirable) behaviors that don't exhibit themselves except in certain circumstances; you don't want to do a couple of simple tests, decide that the old version works just fine, and do a new deployment, only to find that any time a visitor adds a third bullet point to a list, the whole page goes to hell.

That's why I suggest that you do all of this on a development box rather than mess with your live site.

Of course, if you've got source code control in place, you'll be deploying to a staging server, where users can test and sign off, and then deploy from there to production, and be able to revert in the case of failure.

Deploy

Once your development box has a fully functioning wiki using the new version of DokuWiki as well as updated versions of templates and plugins, it's time to deploy. This is a simple matter of copying the files from your development installation to the production server.

Now, you may be thinking, "What about my configuration and data? Won't those be overwritten?" And the answer is... no! For example, DokuWiki config files are named

```
conf\acl.auth.php.dist
conf\local.php.dist
conf\users.auth.php.dist
```

and when you modify them, yours are named

```
conf\acl.auth.php
conf\local.php
conf\users.auth.php
```

These files never come with DokuWiki and thus your version are never overwritten.

Data customization

Finally, data! Similarly, the DokuWiki data pages are

```
data\pages\wiki\dokuwiki.txt
data\pages\wiki\syntax.txt
data\pages\wiki\welcome.txt
```

while your data pages are named

```
data\pages\start.txt
data\pages\sidebar.txt
data\pages\task_list.txt.
```

Thus the /data folder (and its various subdirectories (namespaces), if any) can be included in the copy.

Once you've copied the data folder hierarchy, you may want to delete all of the files and folders (except "dummy.txt") in the cache subfolder. Not doing do can sometimes generate problems with pages rendering improperly in the new installation. If there aren't any files in 'cache', then DokuWiki can't get confused about where to get a page from. (See Chapter 10 about how the cache works.)

You can also get rid of any old lock files in the 'locks' folder as well.

If those messages continue to appear

Suppose that you've carefully followed every step in this procedure, but the next time you log in to the wiki, the "An upgrade is available" message(s) still display at the top of every page. Arrghhh!

Here's what's happening. The "conf/msg" file contains, as it's first line, a number. For example, here's what the file contained at the beginning of 2009:

```
14
The first line of this file contains a number, indicating
which notification messages should not be displayed. This
is the only information sent to dokuwiki.org when the
updatecheck option is enabled. You usually don't need to
change this number as it gets updated when you install the
new release - but to ignore a certain message set its
number here.
```

Each message that displays at the top of a page, be it an upgrade notification or a security warning, has a unique ID shown in square brackets:

```
New upgrade available: 2008-05-05 [14]
```

Only messages which have a higher ID than the one configured in "conf/msg" will be shown. When you upgrade to the release announced in the message, the "conf/msg" file will be upgraded as well (by copying the upgrade's version of "conf/msg" over the copy on your production server), suppressing the message. If you don't want to upgrade to an announced release, you can manually edit "conf/msg" and simply increase the number to match the number of the message you want to inhibit from displaying.

So if the message on the page says [21], "conf/msg" will have a number of 20 or lower. To get rid of the messages, change "conf/msg" to read 21.

However, there's a catch! Immediately after upgrading (say, for the next day or so), the upgrade message might still be displayed. DokuWiki caches the "conf/msg" file for a day and will only refetch if the "last modified" timestamp of "conf/msg" is higher than the "last modified" timestamp of the "conf/msg" file in the cache. To deal with this, you can either 1) wait a day, 2) modify the "last modified" timestamp of "conf/msg" (*nix's "touch" command works well for this, or 3) delete data/cache/messages.txt.

14: Using DokuWiki As A Software Developer

So you now know everything you need in order to manage your wiki. But that was all preparation for this chapter: what goes on your wiki. There are many sources and repositories of information for an application, and the wiki is the home base that organizes all of those disparate pieces.

What's most important is to enable your users to find information. This chapter, then, brings it all together, and discusses how to design the sidebar – the table of contents for all those pieces – for your wiki, and examples of what goes on each of those pages.

If you're an abstract thinker, you've already read enough, you probably already have an outline formulated in your mind, how you're going to organize the material on your wiki. But I'm an empirical guy. I need to see examples.

Organizing data is a complex topic, entire branches of study have been formed on how to classify, subdivide, and organize bodies of knowledge. This is no different. After implementing wikis for customers for the last ten years or so, I've found that the topics needed for a software development wiki can be grouped into about a half dozen general areas.

1. Project Management
2. Software Development Tools
3. Reference
4. Development Processes
5. Data
6. How To...
7. Functional Docs

Note that they're not all needed for every project. This list is a smorgasbord of topics from which you can pick and choose as you see fit for your particular needs.

Let's look at them one at a time.

1. Project Management

Every system has some need for project management pages on the wiki. The larger the project, the more likely project management will be handled by a separate software application, but even those can be linked to from a master 'project management' page found on the wiki.

I've found three general types of project management tools are often useful – a task list, a status page, and a project plan. As these are the 'Go To' items for every wiki, I put them at the top of the sidebar, and don't even use a heading on the sidebar. See **Figure 1**.

Hentzenwerke Publishing, Inc.
books@hentzenwerke.com • www.hentzenwerke.com

Figure 1. *Sidebar showing project management links.*

One or more of these answers the question "What's the big picture?"

Task List

This page provides a tabular view of discrete To Do items for the system. Depending on the system, I've found two variations to be useful.

Applications in Development

Applications that are built from scratch have a natural progression of tasks that can be charted and managed by formal project management software and a variety of current software development processes. However, not everyone goes to that extent to do so; many organizations use more of a 'shoot from the hip' style.

Still, even they can benefit from a master list of tasks, such as shown in **Figure 2**.

Task List

(Rubric for new task descriptions)

Date	Done	Resp	Description	Status	Notes
17/6/25		BR	Beta 1	Not started	Sls Mgt only
17/6/20		BR	Create and demo UI prototype	Not started	Decide on libraries, possible new version from Ed and Candi if on time
17/6/16		BR	Outline test plans	In progress	w/o users
17/6/16		AJ	Flesh out domain restrictions	In progress	Core tables only
17/6/16	17/6/18	AJ	Initial data load	Complete	Gym to supply CSV
17/6/10	17/6/17	OO	Install new tables in PostgreSQL	Complete	Admin and user
17/5/28	17/6/16	AJ	Define table structure	Complete	Use salesforce schema

Figure 2. *Sample Task List for module in development.*

This shows a list of tasks in process and completed for a single module of the system.

The columns include:

- **Date** – The date the task was added to the list.

- **Done** – The date the task was completed.
- **Resp** – The person who is responsible for the work for the task.
- **Description** – A brief description of the task. This field is a link to a separate page, where full details can be provided.
- **Status** – A standardized phrase describing where the task is – not started, in progress, complete. Sometimes I include who is currently working on the task.
- **Notes** – A brief synopsis of the status of the task.

The underlying markup behind the table looks like this:

```
^Date ^Done ^Resp ^Description    ^Status       ^Notes ^
|17/6/25 |   |BR   |[[Beta 1]]    |Not started |Sls Mgt only |
```

Clicking on the Description link opens a separate page with whatever details are necessary for the task. The description may range from a free form description to a pre-defined outline for work.

If a standard description page is needed in the project, I will include a link to a blank rubric (or template) for the page in order to help visitors create each new page the same way – see the link at the top of the page, under the 'Task List' heading.

Applications in Maintenance

Applications that are being modified or maintained often have a lot of start and stop, as those tasks are intermittently assigned and delayed, and aren't as often tracked by project management techniques.

As a result, it can be tricky to remember where you left off if work has been suspended for a while. Additionally, if you're trying to accumulate knowledge about an app that you've been brought in to maintain, you will want to log what you have done on previous tasks.

A task list page for these types of applications is absolutely invaluable. On every maintenance project I've ever worked on, we've found ourselves going back to the task list, sometimes years ago, to look up reminders on what we had done on a similar task, for clues on a new issue we're dealing with.

Again, the Task List is a table, with one task per row, as shown in **Figure 3**.

Task List

(Rubric for new task descriptions)

Date	Task #	App	Description	Status	Current Resp
17/12/28	237	LX, LA, C7	Implement new SMTP email server	In process	Dev w/o C7 steps
17/3/26	223	LX	Set Term Date for Life Insurance	To test	JA to test (Bld 6250)
16/4/8	174	LX	Add process to convert HIPAA file to maxCOBRA format	To test	JA to test (Bld 6199)
15/9/26	139	LX	FirstData custom export for south region	In process	TLR to examine file
15/9/20	135	C7	Bank download not clearing banking info in host	In process	w/o bank update
15/7/28	128	LX	maxCOBRA direct payment daily file	In process	JA to test (Bld 6154)

Figure 3. *Task list for unrelated tasks across multiple systems.*

As tasks come up, add them sequentially at the top, so the oldest task is at the bottom. I've found it useful to maintain two tables, one for tasks that are either in progress or yet to be started, and a second table for tasks that are completed. This second table is below the first one on the page, and is kept for historical purposes.

Let's look at the columns in this table. You'll not see a 'Done' column, because the tasks that are completed are moved to a separate table.

- **Date** – Like the previous task list, this is the date that the task is added to the list. As you can see from Figure 3,
- **Task #** - As tasks are added, they're numbered sequentially. The purpose is to be able to refer to tasks later without confusion. It often happens that visitors will use descriptions that aren't distinct enough to use them later.
- **App** – With some companies, there are multiple systems being managed, or the system is large enough that separate modules need to be identified.
- **Description** - A brief description of the task. This field is a link to a separate page, where full details can be provided.
- **Status** - A standardized phrase describing where the task is – not started, in progress, complete. Since the next column includes who's involved, that's all.
- **Current Resp** – Since these tasks can range wildly across systems and there could be a lot of people involved, it helped to explicitly identify who was next up, and what they were doing.

The underlying markup in the page looks like this:

```
^Date     ^Task # ^App ^Description     ^Status      ^Current Resp ^
|17/12/28|237     |LX  | [[SMTP server]] |In process |Dev w/o C7 steps |
```

As tasks are completed, the column can be filled in, but the row remains. This then creates a reminder of what you've done and where you're headed, and it's easier to get rolling again, than if you simply had a single "To Do" item in this section.

Status

Similar, but not identical, to a Task List is a status page. While Tasks are specific To Do items, work on a project may well be organized other ways. For example, a traditional LAN fat-client development project may have a pre-defined menu structure, with forms, reports, and processes being called from each menu bar. A status page might list every function on the menu, and simply list the progress that's been made, so that a casual observer could quickly see the current state of the entire system. See **Figure 4**.

Status

Module Name	Under Construction	In Beta	Feature Complete	Comments
Startup	2016/11/24	12/16	02/10	
Choose Initial Action	2016/12/01	12/29	02/10	
Create New Client	2017/01/04	01/12	02/10	
Create New Factor Definition	2017/01/13	02/20	04/21	
Factor Summary	2017/01/29	03/16	04/21	
Factor 1 - Census	2017/04/16	06/10	06/29	
Factor 1 - Choose Census Area	2017/05/01	06/10	06/29	
Factor 2 - Internal	2017/07/09	08/21	10/04	
Factor 2 - Feeder Selection	2017/07/31	09/15	11/04	
Factor 2 - Feeder Weight	2017/10/02	11/16	12/30	
Factor 3 - Manual	2017/12/06	01/31		
Switch Client	2017/12/20	02/02		Define 'phantom' client
Configure Clients	2018/01/19	03/10		
Point to Census Location	2018/02/15			Need to remove State from Metro opb
Create Custom Areas				W/o design for initialization

Figure 4. *A sample Status page.*

The table in Figure 4 shows columns in a simple status page. These columns include:

- **Module Name** – However the app is broken down into pieces, each row represents a specific deliverable.
- **Under Construction** – When work on a module starts, the date is entered into this column.
- **In Beta** – Once a module has been delivered to the users for testing, the date is entered into this column.
- **Feature Complete** – Once a module has been accepted by the users, the date is entered into this column.

- **Comments** – While not a place for detailed notes, this column is handy for quick remarks about the status of the module

The underlying markup in the page looks like this:

```
^Module                 ^Under          ^In     ^Feature  ^Comments ^
^Name                   ^Construction ^Beta   ^Complete ^          ^
|Startup                |2016/11/24    |12/16 |02/10    |          |
|Choose Initial Action  |2016/12/01    |12/29 |02/10    |          |
```

As modules are finished, dates are filled in across the row. Not intended to be a robust planning tool, this table gives the visitor a birds-eye view of the system.

Project Plan/Schedule

How are you organizing the work to be done on this project? More importantly, how are you communicating and disseminating that information? This isn't a Status Page, that's both a historical document and a current snapshot of the project.

A Project Plan attempts to describe the future – what's going to happen when. So instead of of leaving the milestone columns blank until the event occurs, they're all filled in at once, identifying the dates for the plan.

While any customer who wanted a project plan in that amount of detail used separate project management software, it's possible that your customer wants a simpler solution that would be satisfied by a simple wiki page.

Summary

The one downside of using a table on a wiki page is that they're not as easily manipulated as other dedicated tools. A spreadsheet, for example, has simple column and row hiding functions, sorting capabilities, and many more possibilities in features as, say, a spreadsheet, with its myriad features. But they're easily maintained and provide a community editable, single source of the information everyone wants.

2. Software Development Tools

This next section provides a place to handle the nuts and bolts of software development. While many development teams have discrete systems in place for various components of the process, such as version control and bug reporting, a surprising number of teams are still stuck in the dark ages, where 'version control' consists of a folder full of zip files and 'bug tracking' ends up being a mishmash of emails, voice messages and scraps of paper left on top of the monitor of the developer.

For those cases, using a wiki to centralize these things are a first and critically important step to modernizing the process. See **Figure 5** for an example of how they fit into the sidebar.

You are here: start

Trace: · source · test_plans · 18 · 15 · 14 · 6 · af

Task List
Status
Project Plan

Dev Tools
Builds
Source
Test Plans
AFI List

Welcoi

1. Use
2. To c

ΓΓsa

Figure 5. *Sidebar showing Development Tools links.*

Builds

While it's common for a customer to provide remote access for you so that you can install and update your software, there may be cases where this isn't possible, either for security reasons or for infrastructure constraints. Or even simply because the customer has just never seen the need – they were good with getting a diskette in the mail, and now feel that instant email is a perfectly fine replacement for that archaic and slow moving process.

If you're providing builds, and your customer doesn't have, or give you access to, source code control, you may need an intermediate location for storage. Instead of just emailing files with names like "new build.zip" and "update to tuesday.zip" (both of which I've actually seen from customers), using a centralized location for every update means consistency and reliability. Not quite as useful as version control, where builds can be rolled back, but having a single source means you can go back and investigate issues without having to dig through emails, wondering just when and where that one file was and what was included in it.

A sample Builds page is shown in **Figure 6**.

Builds

Build 91:

Build 91 (2016/2/21)
Updates for Analyzer source code (2016/2/21)

  * AFI 36 In factor.moveF2feeder(), initialized Available based on system defaults.
  * AFI 46 Changed factor.assignF2lblFeederExistence() to set label colors to red if there are feeders and black if there aren't.

Build 90:

Build 90 (2016/1/21)
Complete refresh of Analyzer source code (2016/1/21)

  * AFI 29 Added Next/Prev buttons to JG combo on FS tab of Factor form
  * AFI 30 Added "Return to FS" button that displays on all non-FS tabs
  * AFI 45 Turned Weight column off in Weighting listbox of F2 when 'Unweighted' is selected

Figure 6. *Sample Builds page.*

The Builds page in Figure 6 has a section for each build. First, there are two links per build that download files. The first is the executable file (or files); the second is the supporting source code. Depending on the structure of source code trees, you may want to provide partial source code files with each build and a full source code collection intermittently.

Under the links are descriptions of what changes have been made in the build; these may include source code changes as well as descriptions of the changed functionality.

The underlying markup looks something like this:

```
**Build 91:**\\

{{:wiki:analyzer2.0.091.zip|Build 91 (2016/2/21)}}\\
{{:wiki:source_20160221.zip|Updates for Analyzer source code
(2016/2/21)}}\\

  * AFI 36 In factor.moveF2feeder(), initialized Available based on
system defaults.
  * AFI 46 Changed factor.assignF2lblFeederExistence() to set label
colors to red if there are feeders and black if there aren't.

**Build 90:**\\

{{:wiki:analyzer2.0.090.zip|Build 90 (2016/1/21)}}\\
{{:wiki:source_20160121.zip|Complete refresh of Analyzer source code
(2016/1/21)}}

  * AFI 29 Added Next/Prev buttons to JG combo on FS tab of Factor form
  * AFI 30 Added "Return to FS" button that displays on all non-FS tabs
  * AFI 45 Turned Weight column off in Weighting listbox of F2 when
'Unweighted' is selected
```

Depending on the length of the project and the frequency with which builds are created (daily, or more often, perhaps?) and source code updates are provided, this page can get long.

At times I've archived older builds off to a subsidiary page, as shown in **Figure 7**.

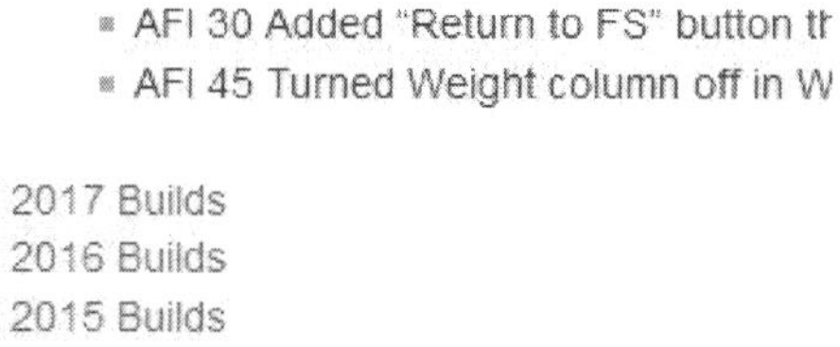

- AFI 30 Added "Return to FS" button th
- AFI 45 Turned Weight column off in W

2017 Builds
2016 Builds
2015 Builds

Figure 7. *Links to pages of older builds.*

If you think that it's a possibility that you'll be archiving off pages and pages of builds, you may choose to create sub-folders for each year of builds.

Source

Depending on the type of and frequency of builds, you may want a separate page for source code.

Depending on the source code tree structure and frequency of builds, you may also want both full source trees as well as interim files that have been changed.

Test Plans

While TDD and automated test suites are all the rage, they're not always possible. On top of that, for smaller, less sophisticated organizations, testing is virtually always an afterthought, if at all. While a chore, a centralized repository of test routines goes a long way in helping recursive testing get done.

Here's where this information goes.

AFI List

There are a number of free, web-based bug tracking systems, some more robust than others. That said, like the other items in this section, it's not hard to find organizations whose idea of bug tracking is a clipboard hung on the wall of the developer that contains a haphazard and usually incomplete list of problems users have run into.

The AFI ("Application Feedback Incident", since bugs are just one type of contact we get from users) list is the master repository for all messages from users, so that everyone can determine what's been reported, the status of each item, and the details of the item – including a description, steps to reproduce, actual results and expected results.

The AFI list is a table, just like the project management pages, with each row representing a single issue. See **Figure 8**.

AFI List

AFI #	Prior ity	Module Name	Date Added	Ready For Test	Tested	Done	Resp	Title
18		Client Config Add	12/21/2017	1/11			JL	Show 'no path chosen' in ee data path r/o textbox
15		Client Config Add	9/29/2014	9/29	10/5	10/16	TO	New client add should create all files if they don't exist
14		Client Config Add	9/28/2014	10/16	10/16	10/16	JL	If fields are missing, they're added, but messagebox isn't clear
6		Client Config Add	6/14/2014	10/16	10/16	10/16	JL	Add Client allows Done w/o Save

Figure 8. *AFI list.*

The columns contain typical bug tracking attributes.

- **AFI #** - As AFIs are added, they're numbered sequentially. Even more so than Tasks, it's critical to be able to uniquely identify an AFI being discussed. The AFI number is a link to a separate wiki page, like the description column on the Task page.
- **Priority** – Depending on the volume of AFIs, there may be a need to prioritize which issues get addressed first.
- **Module Name** – The area of the system that the AFI belongs to. Often a menu item or function on a form.
- **Date Added** – The date that the AFI was added.
- **Ready for Test** – The date that the AFI was turned over by development to whoever does testing – test team or users.
- **Tested** – When the AFI has been tested. In the cases that the issue hasn't been fixed to the satisfaction of the tester, this gets filled in, but the Done column is not, which is a signal for development to address again.
- **Done** – If the AFI has been addressed to the tester's satisfaction, it's marked as done. To be sure, sometimes you may want another column indicating that the change has been put into production.
- **Resp** – The name of the developer or tester who is to do the next segment of work.
- **Title** – A brief description of the AFI. So that it can be easily identified.

The underlying markup for this table looks something like this (broken into two pieces, because the table is wide):

```
^ AFI^Prior^Module        ^Date      ^Ready     ^Tested ^Done
^  #^ity^Name              ^Added     ^For Test ^        ^
|[[18]]| |Client Config Add |12/21/2017 |1/11      |       |
|[[15]]| |Client Config Add |9/29/2014 |9/29      |10/5  |10/16
|[[14]]| |Client Config Add |9/28/2014 |10/16     |10/16 |10/16
|[[6]] | |Client Config Add |6/14/2014 |10/16     |10/16 |10/16
```

Right side of table:

```
^Resp  ^Title ^
^      ^      ^
|JL    |Show 'no path chosen' in ee data path r/o textbox |
```

```
|TO   |New client add should create all files if they don't exist |
|JL   |If fields are missing, they're added, but msgbox isn't clear |
|JL   |Add Client allows Done w/o Save |
```

You'll see that the AFI # in the first column is a link to a separate page, much like Task List descriptions open to a page that describes the task in detail. See **Figure 9**.

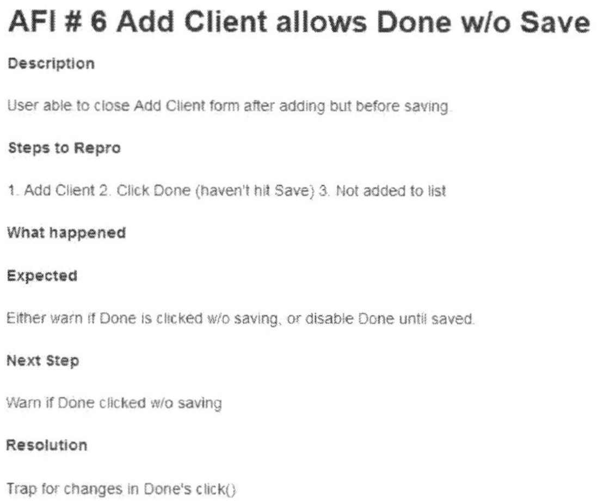

AFI # 6 Add Client allows Done w/o Save

Description

User able to close Add Client form after adding but before saving

Steps to Repro

1. Add Client 2. Click Done (haven't hit Save) 3. Not added to list

What happened

Expected

Either warn if Done is clicked w/o saving, or disable Done until saved.

Next Step

Warn if Done clicked w/o saving

Resolution

Trap for changes in Done's click()

Figure 9. A typical detail page for an AFI.

As AFIs are completed, the columns are filled in. Depending on the length of the list, AFIs that are finished may be split off into their own table, as suggested in the Task List page.

3. Reference

This section is where you put all those things that you'll refer back to, but are 'not elsewhere categorized'. All systems acquire materials that users, in their desire to help, provide, even though there's no rhyme or reason to what they decided to write down and send.

The Reference section sidebar shows a different style, where there are links for some sections, but also a non-linked heading followed by are secondary links. See **Figure 10**.

Figure 10. Reference Files sidebar.

The Files and Glossary links go straight to pages, while the Infrastructure heading is simply a heading for the subsidiary links, Network Info and Folder Structure. The markup supporting this section looks like this:

```
**Reference**\\
[[Files]]\\
[[Glossary]]\\
Infrastructure\\
- [[Network Info]]\\
- [[Folder Structure]]\\
```

Note that the hyphens in front of the Network Info and Folder Structure links aren't included in the brackets.

Resource/Supporting files

Human beings are messy, and iterative development is similarly messy. There are always a variety of documents that are part of that process. It's a good idea to provide a centralized repository for those documents, and the wiki is the perfect place. There typically isn't an orderly list of documents that look like they just came out of the card catalog of an anal-retentive librarian. Rather, the supporting documents resemble the locker of a senior on the last day of high school.

Still, it's possible to put this pile into a bit of order. Your users will likely provide you with documents with random names like "west sales.docx", "screens.xlsx", and a series of "order process 3", "order process 4", "order 5", and "maintain order version 6". It's difficult to keep those in any semblance of order, much less try to find them later. If you tried to upload them to the Reference page on the wiki, you'd end up with a page marked up looked like this:

```
{{ ::west sales.docx |}}\\
{{ ::screens.xlsx |}}\\
{{ ::order process 3.docx |}}\\
{{ ::order process 4.doc |}}\\
{{ ::order 5.docx |}}\\
{{ ::maintain_order_version6.docx |}}\\
```

and the result would look like that shown in **Figure 10**.

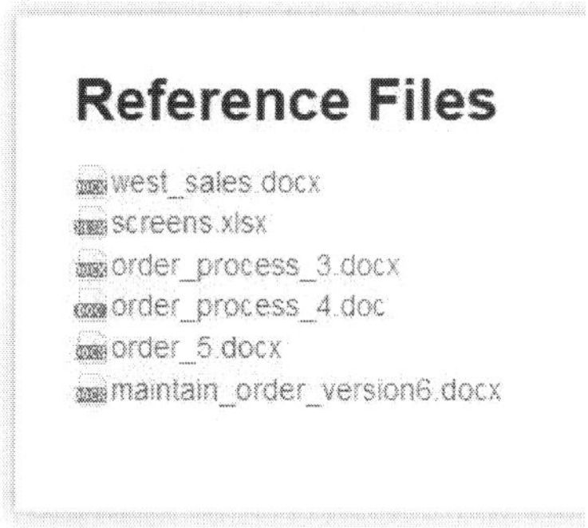

Reference Files

west_sales.docx
screens.xlsx
order_process_3.docx
order_process_4.doc
order_5.docx
maintain_order_version6.docx

Figure 10. Randomly named and organized reference files.

I have three suggestions to deal with this cacophony of ill-considered names. First, organize the reference documents according to function. When you're building a specification, users will often provide descriptions of processes, lists of data, and screen shots and other information about the interface. So break out the documentation according to their function.

Second, use DokuWiki's ability to link to a file and provide a more descriptive label for that link.

And finally, include the date of the document in the link.

Incorporating all three of these suggestions would use markup like this:

```
** Data and Lists **

{{ ::west sales.docx |Western Division Sales Reps}} (2017/11/06)\\

** Interface **

{{ ::screens.xlsx |List of Unused Screens in Finance Dept}}
(2017/10/10)\\

** Processes **
```

```
{{ ::order process 3.docx |Order Maintenance Process v3}}
(2015/01/16)\\
{{ ::order process 4.doc |Order Maintenance Process v4}} (2016/11/06)\\
{{ ::order 5.docx |Order Maintenance Process v5}} (2017/04/29)\\
{{ ::maintain_order_version6.docx |Order Maintenance Process v6}}
(2017/06/18)\\
```

And the resulting reference page would look like that shown in **Figure 11**.

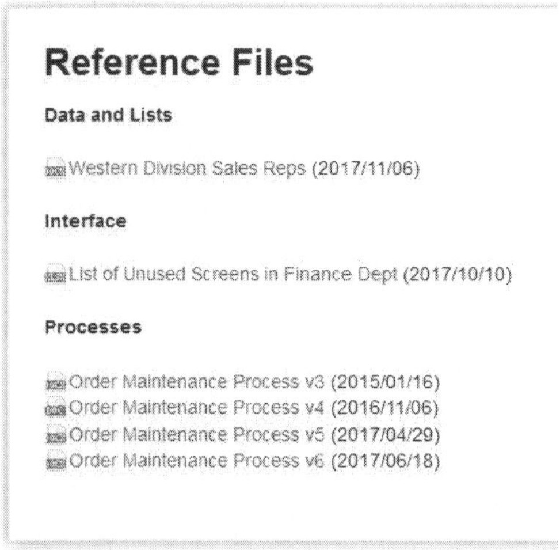

Reference Files

Data and Lists

Western Division Sales Reps (2017/11/06)

Interface

List of Unused Screens in Finance Dept (2017/10/10)

Processes

Order Maintenance Process v3 (2015/01/16)
Order Maintenance Process v4 (2016/11/06)
Order Maintenance Process v5 (2017/04/29)
Order Maintenance Process v6 (2017/06/18)

Figure 11. A much better version of the reference files page.

Other enhancements you might consider:
- include the name of the person from whom the file came, in order to keep the etymology of the file clear.
- use use the tables markup to create two or more columns of files if you wish.

Glossary/Nomenclature

In many industries and companies, there is a whole suite of terminology that is particular to that industry and/or company. This is the place to define those terms so that you can make sure you and your customer are communicating correctly. There's the famous line about "If you call a tail a leg, how many legs does a dog have?" "Five." "No, a dog still has four legs. Calling a tail a leg does not make it a leg."

It's best to describe each one of these terms and define what they mean. Don't just use a description of that term—provide live examples. This ensures that you really do understand what they mean and you're not making incorrect assumptions.

Suppose you're describing an entity that receives medical care at an urgent care facility. If you simply describe that entity as "people" or "patients," you haven't made clear a possible distinction between insured individuals and dependents of an insured individual. However, if you then provide an example of an individual and their entire family as being maintained in the same screen, your intent and plans for overloading the person table with both insureds and dependents becomes obvious.

Infrastructure

This next section has to do with the technical specifications of the supporting infrastructure. As with software, hardware often evolves and the documentation of what's been put in place never seems to keep up. Users have limited and imperfect views of what's in place, and the IT guys live with it day in and day out, so it's all in their heads (or should be).

Needing just enough knowledge about the hardware and network to build software to run on it falls somewhere in between. Here's the place to document what you have found out so that you can refer back instead of having to try and remember.

Network Info

Before we begin talking about the individual system (or systems), we need to have the lay of the land, that is, the configuration of the network. Ideally there's a network or systems administrator who can provide this information, else maybe an outside consulting firm who manages the network on an as-needed basis.

You'll want a network diagram, specifically the server as well as the relevant workstations, and perhaps how the network is connected to the outside world. You'll also want machine descriptions, IP addresses, permissions, and logins.

Are there SQL databases or other servers on the network that are needed? Connection strings, credentials, where those resources are located, how they're backed up.

If the application isn't self-contained on the company's network, you'll need URLs, usernames, passwords to outside resources.

Depending on the complexity of the network, you'll also want a description of the relevant folder structures and contents on the server and workstations.

Folder Structure

Many organizations – and not just small companies – have little to no control over their company servers. Without a well thought-out and maintained set of user controls, users are prone to create folders left and right, leaving a trail of randomness that nobody understands.

Here is where you document the high level folder structure of the network servers, together with what they're used for. The primary purpose of this documentation is to identify where the pieces of the system – development, test and production components – reside.

4. Development Process

This section is for documenting how to use the development tools to build and maintain the system. See **Figure 12** for the main links.

- Network Info
- Folder Structure

Development
Production
Dev Environment
Dev Process
Testing in Dev
Testbed Environment

Data

Figure 12*. Development sidebar links.*

While it might seem to make sense to start with source code and traverse the development cycle until you've placed a build into production, we really need to know where we're heading first. It's been my experience that you want to have just what you're aiming for pinned down first – the executable and production environment that the users are actually using now.

While a lot of this will be straightforward, indeed, even trivial, if you're the one who has built the system, the following both provides a rubric for you to follow when documenting for those who will follow you as well as if you're charged with investigating a system that you've inherited. And sometimes you finish a project only to have the client call back years later, so you might be the poor developer who needs some hints. Much of the tone of the following is aimed at that latter scenario, so don't take offense if you're the developer.

Production Environment

All too often, your users will have simply the vaguest of ideas of just what they're using. "We just click on the X icon on the desktop" or, worse, the application is loaded automatically when they log into their computer. They may well have no idea of what they're doing past their little window into the application. It'll be up to you to figure out the details, so get out your Sherlock Holmes hat, magnifying glass, and ring up Dr. Watson, because the game is afoot.

I'll assume that you have a primary contact at the company, and they have a basic understanding of the system, what it's purpose is, and will be able to point you to who uses 'the system'. It's time to answer the basic Who, How, Where, and What questions.

Who

So this is the first step – who uses the system and, how do they access it?

Very likely they just click on an icon on the desktop, or perhaps there's a menu option in the Windows Start menu, or it's possible that the program loads automatically. And that's assuming it's a desktop program – what if you're documenting a Web-based application? In that case, it'd likely be a URL, either public or on a private intranet. And the mechanism would be yet different again if you're documenting a tablet or smartphone application.

While beyond the scope of this wiki-centric book to discuss all the possibilities, and the myriad technical machinations behind them, ultimately we come down to the same thing – a user is running a main program of one sort or another. It's critical to realize from the outset that the startup process may vary from user to user, so you need to define who the entire user base is, and run through the next step for multiple users.

How

So we know that a user is running a main program of one sort or another. You need to locate and define the steps the user performs to run that program, and how the user executes it, together with any custom parameters that vary from user to user.

Where

Now that you've got the user(s) and the steps they take, we start to come to the part that's interesting to us as developers – where are the executables (or other programs)? I included the parenthetical clause because it's still possible, in this day and age, that users are not running a true executable (.EXE) with runtime files. If the system is old, they very well may have been set up with the program running through a masked IDE or other pseudo-development environment. As a result, you may not be looking for EXEs, but rather interpreted files that are being executed on the fly.

What

Now it's time for the last, and arguably most crucial, question: Where is the data that the programs are working with?

One would think that this would be simple, that everyone running a system would know where the database(s) are, but sadly, this is often a mystery. To be sure, they'll likely have a rough idea, or they'll know where **some** of the data is, but it's very possible that the former developer was not as fastidious as one would like, and that data is scattered across multiple locations.

Perhaps user logins and other configuration items are located in the same place as the program, but application data is located elsewhere. Perhaps application data is scattered across multiple locations, indeed, I've seen systems where the startup routine points to tables in over a half dozen different folders on multiple drives. And if the system uses a client-server architecture, then there may be one or more SQL server back-ends to locate.

Finally, you'll need to be aware whether the data is transportable. Most legacy systems I've run across have hard-coded paths to the data files in the programs. Bad architecture, for sure, but it happens.

There's a whole separate section in the sidebar for data.

Development Environment

We're almost at the end. Now let's start at the beginning.

Once you know where you are going, you can figure out where you are and how to get there. Again, if you're the developer, much of this will be second nature, but if you're charged with investigating a system that's new to you, much of this will be a mystery. And even if this is your system, if it's in maintenance mode, you may not be spending much time with it anymore, so writing down the basics may prove helpful when you're called back to it a few months hence.

Too often, if you start with the development environment, you'll be tempted to start critiquing what's in place, maybe even starting to make little improvements here and there, and suddenly you've messed up the development environment to the point that you're unable to accomplish that first critical step – ensuring that you can build the executable that's currently in production.

But since we've covered the production environment already, we know where we're headed. Let's dig into the code.

Development Tools

Before you go any further, you might want to check where the master copies of your development environment are. These days, many environments have been installed via electronic downloads, but it's a good idea to document where the originals are, in order to set up a new machine, or replace the machine you're working on.

And not just the environment, but third party tools and other resources. All too easy to have a critical library that's used in just one place, and forgotten about until it a new machine is requisitioned, and that library is found to be missing.

Doing so may force so you to examine the original sources, and see if they're still viable.

How to Load the Development Environment

It never ceases to amaze me how developers take so little time to set up their own environment to make their day to day development easier. As a result, don't assume anything about the way the previous developer gets into their environment.

Indeed, I've seen places where the developer opens the Windows Start menu and navigates through multiple levels of menus to start up their IDE, and then they issue multiple commands to change folders, set paths, and get a project loaded – and they'll do this multiple times an hour. Despite their job being the automation of other people's workflows, the idea of creating a shortcut on the taskbar that points them right to their source code never occurred to them.

Where is the Source Code

As I just mentioned, it wouldn't be unusual to find that the developer who came before you manually set up their environment each time they started up their development program.

That means that you'll have to hunt around for where the source is, and it could be pretty tricky, even if you've got help from them. As I'm writing this chapter, I'm working on two projects where the previous developer had multiple copies of source code in various locations around the server.

Just so you don't get cocky, here's an example of the multitude of source code folders I found at one customer's site (identifiable names have been changed):

```
Machine 0.201

Production\Upgrade Project - AR and Inventory
```

Hentzenwerke Publishing, Inc.
books@hentzenwerke.com • www.hentzenwerke.com

```
Sales\ORDERS\ORDERS
Sales\xORDERS\xORDERS

Machine 1.190 Drive C

Original\DOS\Library
Original\DOS\ORDERS
Original\files\Inventory
LIBRARY
orders
new orders
shipping5
Timeslips
Timeslips_DO NOT USE
Timeslips_DO NOT USE2
UPS connects

Machine 1.192 Drive R

New\orders
New\test\orders
New\xorders
Old\orders
Old\test\orders
Old\xorders
shipping6
UPS dont use
```

Yes, each of these folders is the top level of a source code hierarchy. Want to bet where the most current version of the development source code is?

Build the Executable – Parts 1 and 2

The acid test for determining whether you've found the current source is to build an executable. There are three phases to this process.

The first is whether you can build the executable without error. This can be more challenging that it seems. If you can create a new EXE without error, great, but don't assume that if the process throws errors, you've got problems. The previous developer may have run into errors and just let them go, putting a suspect executable into play. "Yeah, it always does that. Doesn't seem to hurt anything."

The second phase is whether the executable matches the one already in use. Depending on the development toolset in use, you may have access to the internals of the EXE, but at a bare minimum you can compare the file sizes of both executables.

If you can do that, you're not home free. The final phase is to copy what you believe is the current source to a clean machine and do a complete rebuild. If the build completes successfully **and** you again get an executable the same size as the one in production, please email me, because in 25 years of taking over other developer's systems, I've never been able to make this happen the first time through. There's always a set of files squirreled away in another folder somewhere.

DokuWiki: A Wiki For Software Developers

Once you've done all this, document the results in this section. Particular for systems in maintenance mode, this can be helpful down the road.

Development Process

Now that you know where the source is, how do you make changes? The first thing you need to know is how the source code is structured. Once you know that, you can document how to make changes, test, and deploy to production

Background

Is there hidden knowledge about how the system is structured, or how the development process is implemented, that isn't necessarily obvious?

Program Flow

What is the main program? How does the logic to call menu items or whatever other user functions work?

Change Process

Given the morass of source code I've run into over the years, I've found it helpful to write out the steps I take for every change I make. The first few are all bespoke investigations, but eventually a rubric for future changes becomes evident. This is where that rubric belongs, an outline for how to go about the next change.

Testing in Development

One of the strengths of many modern IDEs is that they are truly **interactive**. That is, you can run the system from within the IDE, against a data set, and watch the program run. This capability, surprisingly, is a new concept to an uncomfortably large number of developers. I've lost track of the number of times I've been told that I have to build an executable and put it in a new location to test it.

So you may have to figure out and document how to test interactively, because you may be the first person doing it.

Where is the Test Data for Running Interactively?

If this is the case for the system you're working on, it behooves you to find this out now. If not, find out what data the system is running against. You don't want to be running the system in the IDE only to find out that you're working with live data.

Separate Testbed Environment

Once you've got a new change completed and tested in development, you may move it into a separate staging environment, an infrastructure where they have a copy of the production data and a staging area for test builds to be deployed before moving into actual use.

This environment may be as elegant as a completely separate staging server with segregated data, or as simple as a copy of live data in a test folder and a separate folder to hold the new EXE.

Regardless, if it's available, you'll want to document how to move builds from development into testing.

5. Data

Applications come and go, but data lives forever. And interestingly enough, nobody really knows their data. I can't think of a single customer over 25 years who had a comprehensive handle on what was in their tables, much less how their database was organized. Indeed, most developers don't really remember all the details – we're only human. So as you spelunk through the system, you'll pick up stuff and it behooves you to document what you discover.

There are two basic questions about data: Where is it, and what does it consist of. See **Figure 13**.

Figure 13. *Data sidebar links.*

Data Files

First things first – just where is their data? While some developer are meticulous and methodical, more often you'll find one-off cases where the bulk of the data is in the appropriately named 'db' folder (or 'data' or 'dbases' or 'surveys'), but there always seem to be a few references to files elsewhere.

Maybe there are a couple of tables in the root folder that were supposed to have been moved, but that never quite happened. Perhaps there's an 'output' folder that ended up having some result files that are now used during daily operations. Or a department wants all their data in a different place, because they have another application that also uses some of the data for querying and reporting.

And hopefully, although not likely, they've got both test and live data. One would hope there is some rhyme and reason to the structures, but I've seen some doozies, where live data is in one configuration of folders, and test data is in a different set of folders – and the folder structures aren't the same! The more irregular things are, the more they cry out for documentation.

Data Dictionary

A data dictionary – rather, **the** data dictionary – is a natural item to put on the wiki, so that everyone can access it. Depending on the development tools you're using, you may have an actual data dictionary tool that's integrated with your development environment, but perhaps not. And if you do, it's unlikely that users have access or the skill to use the data dictionary. In either case, it's good to have a single source that describes the data in terms that the users can understand.

If you're in one of those 'Not Invented Here' shops, a simple list of tables and fields in a spreadsheet or document is better than nothing.

6. How To...

My senior year high school science teacher, the advanced physics class, introduced the year the first day by saying, “You know how when you were little you’d ask all those odd questions and your parents would say, ‘don’t bother me with such silly things’? Well, here’s where you get to ask those questions.”

Similarly, this section is where you collect all those tidbits of knowledge from around the system, the tips and tricks that you will inevitably collect while working with the system, but that don’t seem to belong to any specific part of the system.

The software version of the shoebox full of receipts that lands on the accountant’s desk.

How To...
How Things Work
How To...
Troubleshooting

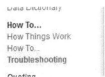

***Figure 14**. How To sidebar.*

How Things Work

This is where you list conceptual parts of the system. Rare is the time that a customer will open their checkbook and say “Go ahead and document every nook and cranny of our system.” So you’ll end up with a smorgasbord of bits and pieces of knowledge acquired intermittently during your investigations. Here’s where those bits and pieces go.

How To...

This page is a collection of links for specific tasks. Each page is an individual set of instructions for that task. It makes sense to group tasks in categories, and add to those categories as needed. The first category I always start with is “Wiki Usage”, since it’s a universal topic across all wikis. I always add “Edit the Sidebar” as the first topic. See **Figure 15**.

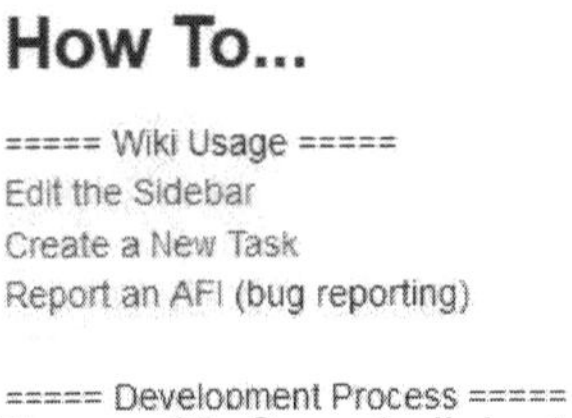

How To...
===== Wiki Usage =====
Edit the Sidebar
Create a New Task
Report an AFI (bug reporting)
===== Development Process =====

***Figure 15**. Sample links to How To topics under the Wiki Usage section.*

Other categories on the How To... page often include

- **Setup Processes** – This is where tasks like configuring a new machine or setting up a new remote desktop configuration go.
- **Development Process** – This is where tasks like finding components in the source code tree, creating a new build, and deploying to production go.
- **User Processes** – Day-to-day use of a system invariably involves routines bordering on folklore, never written down and poorly understood. As you discover these, this is a great place to document them. Especially good to document are those once-a-year, blue-moon processes like archiving and lopping off data when the server fills up, doing the once-a-year journal reset, or setting up a new workstation. Additionally, as you create or modify functions, this is where you can write down how to use those functions.

Troubleshooting

If you're lucky, the users of the system have accumulated a list of 'common problems' and their fixes. As often as not, though, this list is in those people's heads, or on handwritten pages stapled to the side of someone's cubicle.

The wiki, natch, is a great place to centralize all of this.

7. Functional Docs

The final piece to the wiki is documenting what the system does. This is not a technical specification, but a functional one – concentrating on the functions that the user can perform.

Systems are often in a state of flux, sometimes left unfinished as user's eyes outgrew their budget or patience. Documentation is always the last item on the To Do list, so discovery of what actually works, and what those working pieces do, is up to you. This section is where this information goes.

System Inventory

The discussion up to this point has been primarily focused on the technical layout and underpinnings of the system. Now it's time to really look at the system from the user's point of view.

Sometimes a system consists of one program or application, with a main menu which launches everything the users want to do.

Other times, the system consists of a collection of programs, systems, routines, batch files, and so on.

The system inventory is where you list all the components of 'the system' - not just the main application (or applications) that the users see, but also all of the other moving pieces that operate behind the scenes.

Application Menu

Walk through the application's main menu and build a hierarchy of links for each menu pad, menu item, and subsequent sub-menus. A possible menu for the Quoting System at Dynamite Construction Machines might look like this:

```
File
  Quote Maintenance
    Customer Lookup
    Item Lookup
    Print
  Prospect Handling
Processes
  Product Maintenance
    Product Split
    Product Merge
Reports
  Stats
Utilities
```

I've organized this menu with indents for menus and submenus. The File, Processes, Reports and Utilities lines are menu bars across the top, Quote Maintenance and Prospect Handling are menu bars under File, and the three items under Quote Maintenance are submenus off the Quote Maintenance menu bar.

Now, it's easy to indent menus and submensu in a typed list; making that list appear indented on the wiki sidebar is a little more difficult.

If you've been practicing the editing of pages for a bit (per Chapter 9), you know that you can't just tap the space bar a couple of times to create an indent. And you can't use the HTML code for a space ( ) either. Here are some examples of the markup that you might try:

```
  [[Quote Maintenance]]
  [[Quote Maintenance]]
[[- Quote Maintenance]]
```

These variations end up displaying the abominations under the File hyperlink as shown in **Figure 16**.

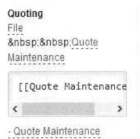

Figure 16. *Various mechanisms to indent a menu item in the sidebar.*

The first and second are obviously unacceptable; the third may or may not be aesthetically pleasing, as shown in **Figure 17**.

Quoting
File
- Quote Maintenance
-- Customer Lookup
-- Item Lookup
-- Print
- Prospect Handling
Processes
- Product
Maintenance
-- Product Split
-- Product Merge
Reports
- Stats
Utilities

Figure 17. *The application menu for the Quoting system.*

While there are a number of tricks to get around these issues, I've found the quickest and easiest to remember is simply a variation of the third choice - using hyphens to indent. A single hyphen for a single indent, two hyphens for a deeper indent, and so on. The sidebar, then, would look like **Figure 18**.

Quoting
File
- Quote Maintenance
– Customer Lookup
– Item Lookup
– Print
- Prospect Handling
Processes
- Product Maintenance
– Product Split
– Product Merge
Reports
- Stats
Utilities

Figure 18. *An alternative method to indent links in the sidebar.*

Being the worldwide conglomerate that it is, Dynamite Construction Machines has other applications, an Order Processing system and an Inventory Management app. Separate sections of the sidebar would be constructed for them, as shown in **Figure 19**.

Quoting
File
- Quote Maintenance
– Customer Lookup
– Item Lookup
– Print
- Prospect Handling
Processes
- Product Maintenance
– Product Split
– Product Merge
Reports
- Stats
Utilities

Order Processing
Order Maintenance
Customer Maintenance
- Combine Accounts
- Customer Scans
Archival

Inventory
Products
- Assembly Analysis
- Station Dispersal
- Maintenance Charting
Scheduling
Reporting

Figure 19. The complete sidebar, including all three systems.

What goes on each of these pages? You most likely will not have time to do a complete specification, so these pages act as placeholders for the information you find out as you work on a particular menu item.

The goal for these pages is to leave breadcrumbs for yourself, so that the next time you need to address that menu item, you can do it more efficiently.

These breadcrumbs can be grouped into two areas.

First, you'll only begin documenting a menu item when there's work to be done on it. That means that you'll have a specific task to perform.

Thus, the first area will be a collection of tasks. A user is reporting a problem or request for a change, and thus will be providing information on how they're using the function – you'll want to document those steps, both as a reminder for review of that task as well as to remind yourself how the function for that menu item works.

The second area will be generally applicable information about the menu item. For example, what source code relates to the menu item. Next, what data is involved. Third, as you trace the operation of the form, report or process, notes on what's going under the hood.

Off the Grid Programs

While the menu traversing is pretty obvious, you should also be aware that there may be standalone programs that interact as well, perhaps routines on a timer, or run off the system scheduler, or separate applications that aren't obvious.

Each of these standalone programs will get their own wiki page, just like each menu item gets its own. Depending on how many there are, you may simply list them down the length of the sidebar, or group them into sections and provide sidebar links for each section, or maybe just have a single link for "Standalone Routines" at the bottom of the sidebar.

Just like the menu items, these will be placeholders until there comes a time that you need to work on one. Once you create the page, you'll break it up into two sections like the menu items – the generally applicable information, such as the name of the routine, how it's accessed, where the source code is, and the specific tasks assigned for that routine.

Other Topics

The areas I've discussed so far are the ones that I've found most useful in my experience. As with everything, your mileage may vary. Other areas that you might find useful include the following:

- **Asset Management** - In the IT field, asset management is the practice of tracking physical and digital assets for the purpose of providing cost-effective level of service. Larger firms universally use dedicated software to manage the volumes of data, but small firms may well use rudimentary systems, such as spreadsheets or documents, if at all. In lieu of no tracking at all, a wiki page listing hardware and software, using simple tables for both, can provide a centralized listing of assets.
- **Ticketing System** – Ticketing systems can be used to track issues on a more sophisticated level than a simple list on a wiki page. If your organization uses one, you may want documentation about and links to your to ticketing system.
- **Resource Support Tools** – Infrastructure requires a variety of support tools, such as management, administration and troubleshooting. You may want to have a master list of tools and associated documentation.
- **On-Call Rotation Schedules** – Some organizations need around the clock support to handle emergency calls, and use an on-call rotation of support personnel to do so. Smaller companies may well use a manually generated and maintained schedule of who is on-call. This schedule can reside on the wiki where everyone can access it.

Hentzenwerke Publishing, Inc.
books@hentzenwerke.com • www.hentzenwerke.com

- **Employee Training** – Organizations may have a formal or informal process of tracking the programs, classes and seminars that employees attend. In lieu of a formal employee training tracking software package, a page on the wiki can serve as a repository for tracking who has done what.
- **Vendor Management** – The skyrocketing complexity of IT infrastructure means that the vendors involved in supporting said infrastructure comprise more than a handful of Rolodex cards. A centralized list of vendors, numbers and associated assets on a wiki page is a start.
- **Contract Management** – Similar to Vendor Management, a centralized list of support contracts with third parties could sit well on a wiki page.
- **Outage Tracking** – While perhaps a bit sophisticated for companies using a wiki for knowledge base topics, if uptime for services are guaranteed, you may have a link for outage tracking software.
- **Change Management** – As organizations become more sophisticated in their handling of software, they become more rigorous in handling changes in software versions. This page is the jumping off point for Software Change (or Configuration) Management tools.
- **Operational Checklists** – There's a reason that checklists are used by pilots with 20 years of experience. Because people forget steps. Even more so when those steps aren't performed on a regular basis. But even the best checklist isn't much good if people can't find it. Here's where you put those checklists.

Sidebar Design Considerations

Now that we've got all this material assembled, how do we put it into our wiki? Specifically, how do we structure the sidebar with all of these links? A sidebar containing every link discussed in this chapter is lengthy, but manageable. However, while the first six sections are fairly fixed in size, the last – the functional specifications for applications – can range wildly in size.

The applications presented here as samples are nearly trivial, with just a couple dozen links. It's easy to come across a mature system with hundreds of links; I've worked on systems with thousands. Clearly, while it's technically possible to put all those on a sidebar, the scrolling needed would wear out mousewheels – and index fingers - in a flash. I did have one customer who insisted on having every component of every screen on the sidebar, resulting in a list with over 600 links. That kind of obviated the benefit of a hyperlink wiki, but it was what they wanted. So what do you do with hundreds of menu items to deal with?

Let's suppose you've got an application with hundreds and hundreds of link (or multiple applications, which when considered together result in the same result.) What are your choices to deal with this multitudinous scenario?

One possibility is to remove the nested levels for the application, just displaying the links for the top level menu pads. The links each navigate to single pages – very long pages, in some cases – that contain all the information for that menu pad. Each menu item and submenu item is identified via headings.

Another possibility is to similarly use the pages that those menu pad links navigate to for pages that display cascading trees of the menu items attached to that menu pad. In other words, create a sort of sidebar on the page for all the menu items under the menu pad.

A third option is for the sidebar links to navigate to pages that contain information just on the main screen, and the discussion on those pages contain links to subsequent pages.

The answer? Of course, 'it depends' - the choice is up to you and your particular situation, as well as the needs of your user base. If the visitors are all regular users of the wiki, it's one thing – they may be able to work with a complex wiki, but if they're just stopping by occasionally, you'll need to keep things very simple.

Hentzenwerke Publishing, Inc.
books@hentzenwerke.com • www.hentzenwerke.com

Hentzenwerke Publishing, Inc.
books@hentzenwerke.com • www.hentzenwerke.com